AIRPLANES

and TRUCKS

and TRAINS,

FIRE ENGINES,

BOATS and SHIPS and

BUILDING and WRECKING MACHINES

by GEORGE ZAFFO

GROSSET & DUNLAP • Publishers • NEW YORK

1977 Printing

ISBN: 0-448-01887-X (TRADE EDITION)
ISBN: 0-448-03186-8 (LIBRARY EDITION)

Library of Congress Catalog Card Number: 68-21295

Copyright 1949, 1950, 1951,
Copyright © 1953, 1958, 1963, 1964, 1966 by Grosset & Dunlap, Inc.
All rights reserved under International and Pan-American Copyright Conventions.
Published simultaneously in Canada.   Printed in the United States of America.

The contents of this book were previously published under the following
titles: The Book of Airplanes; The Big Book of Real Trucks; The Big Book
of Real Trains; The Big Book of Real Fire Engines; The Big Book of Real
Building and Wrecking Machines; and The Big Book of Real Boats and Ships.

AIRPLANES

JET PLANE IN FLIGHT • One of the fastest operational jet airplanes is the Convair Hustler, which weighs 165,000 pounds fully loaded and can fly at 1,385 miles per hour. It has four turbojet engines attached under its wings. The men of the Strategic Air Command call it the B-58A Hustler. This fast bomber, carrying a crew of only three men, can fly 2,500 miles without refueling at an altitude of 60,000 feet. The delta wing enables it to fly faster than planes whose wings are straight. Additional fuel, material or weapons may be contained in a pod under the fuselage. The Hustler's wing span is 56 feet 10 inches; its fuselage is 96 feet 9 inches long; its height is 31 feet 5 inches.

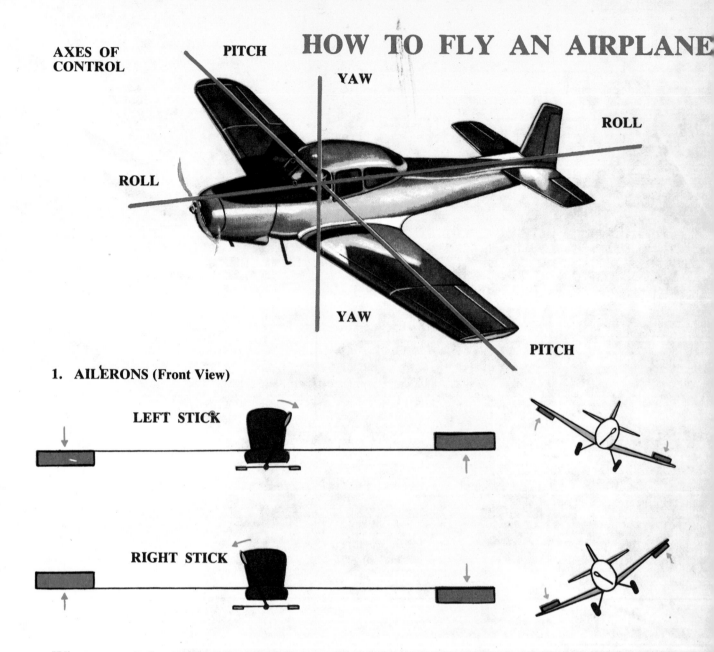

AXES OF CONTROL

PITCH

YAW

ROLL

ROLL

YAW

PITCH

1. AILERONS (Front View)

LEFT STICK

RIGHT STICK

When you sit in an airplane cockpit you see a whole bank of knobs, dials and handles. They look complicated, but the controls that steer the airplane are really very simple to operate. An automobile needs only a steering wheel. It drives on the road and turns only to one side or the other. But an airplane not only turns right or left but also up and down. An airplane operates on three fixed lines, called axes—the axis of pitch, the axis of roll, and the axis of yaw. Movement around the axis of yaw is controlled by the rudder. Movement around the axis of pitch is controlled by the elevators. Movement around the axis of roll is controlled by the ailerons.

There are two ways to make an airplane turn sideways. One way is to move the *ailerons*. The ailerons are little hinged flaps on the back end of each wing. They can be moved up or down by a *control stick* in the cockpit. When the control stick is moved to the right, the aileron on the right wing moves up and the aileron on the left wing moves down. This makes the air blowing over the ailerons push the right wing down—and the airplane starts to turn or *bank* to the right. When the control stick is moved to the left, the left wing is pushed down in just the same way, and the airplane starts turning to the left. The other way to make the airplane turn sideways is to move the *rudder*. The rudder is in the back of the airplane, and it works like the tail of a fish. The rudder is operated by foot pedals. When the right pedal is pushed down, the rudder turns to the right. The wind blows against it and pushes the tail to the left. That makes the nose of the

2. RUDDER (Top View)

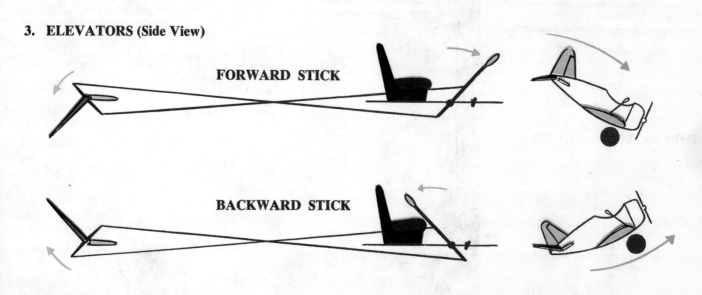

RIGHT RUDDER

LEFT RUDDER

3. ELEVATORS (Side View)

FORWARD STICK

BACKWARD STICK

plane turn to the right. The nose turns to the left when the left rudder pedal is pushed down. An airplane turns best when both the control stick and the rudder pedals are pushed at the same time, since they work together.

There are also two ways to make the plane go up and down. One way is to move the *elevator*. The elevator is a little hinged flap set crosswise in the tail. The same control stick which moves the ailerons also operates the elevator. When the control stick is pushed forward, the elevator moves down. The air blows against it and pushes the tail up. This makes the nose of the airplane point down. Then the plane starts to go down. When the control stick is pulled backward, the tail is pushed down, and the nose of the plane points up. Then the plane starts to climb. The other way to make the plane go up or down is to make the engine and propeller turn faster. The engine is controlled by the *throttle*—just as in an automobile. When the throttle is pushed in, the engine turns faster. Then the airplane starts to climb. When the throttle is pulled out, the engine runs slower and the airplane starts to descend. The throttle is also used to make the airplane go faster or slower, of course. So you see a plane can be steered through the air with only three controls. They are the control stick, used much like the steering wheel of a car, the rudder pedals, and the throttle. It is a little harder to fly an airplane than to drive an automobile, but not much harder. Maybe you'll be a pilot someday!

TWIN CO-AXIAL ROTORS

TWIN INTERMESHED ROTORS

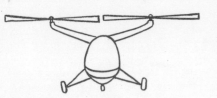

TWIN OUTBOARD ROTORS

TWIN TANDEM ROTORS

DIFFERENT WAYS TO MOUNT TWIN ROTORS

THE HELICOPTER • Helicopters cannot fly as fast as airplanes, but they can do some things that airplanes cannot do: they can land straight down or take off straight up. Helicopters do not have wings. Instead, they have two sets of propellers, called *rotors,* that whirl around very fast and lift the machines right off the ground. Most helicopters have one big rotor overhead and a small rotor in the tail. The tail rotor helps the pilot steer the helicopter and keep it going in the right direction. If there were no tail rotor, the helicopter would spin around opposite to the movement of its overhead rotor. The big overhead rotor lifts the helicopter straight up or

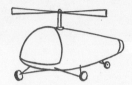

**SINGLE ROTOR
AND TAIL ROTOR**

**SINGLE ROTOR
JET REACTION TAIL**

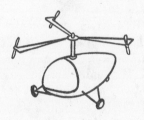

**SINGLE ROTOR
JET-PROPELLED BLADES**

**SINGLE ROTOR
PROPELLERS ON BLADES**

DIFFERENT WAYS TO MOUNT SINGLE ROTORS

lets it come down straight. It also helps it move ahead through the air, because when the rotor blade is turning, it takes a bigger "bite" through the air on its way back than it does when moving forward. (A canoe paddle in water works the same way.) Some helicopters have two big overhead rotors and no tail rotors. Each of the big rotors helps lift the helicopter and move it forward. Such helicopters do not need tail rotors to keep them from spinning, because the overhead rotors turn in opposite directions and balance each other. The picture shows helicopters picking up supplies from an aircraft carrier for combat troops on land.

PARTS OF AN AIRPLANE

1. Ailerons	7. Wing	12. Landing Gear	17. Wing Span
2. Trailing Edge	8. Leading Edge	13. Tail Light	18. Cabin
3. Fuselage	9. Windshield	14. Wing-Tip	19. Landing Light
4. Elevators	10. Jet Pod	Fuel Tank	20. Cabin Door
5. Rudder	11. Horizontal	15. Air Intake	
6. Fin	Stabilizer	16. Jet Thrust	

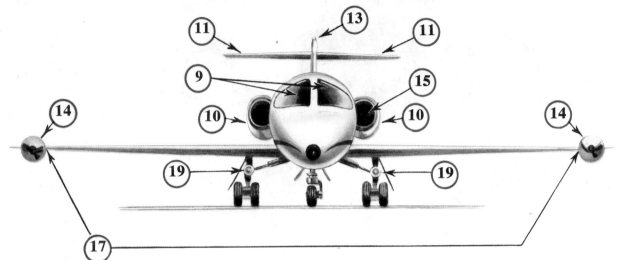

AERONAUTICAL TERMS

AILERON. A section of the rear edge of the airplane wing, which has hinges to help make the airplane turn.

AIRPLANE. An aircraft with fixed wings, which is heavier than the air and is driven by an engine.

AIRPORT. A place where airplanes land and take off. It usually has hangars where airplanes can be housed, and buildings for passengers and freight.

AIRSHIP. A lighter-than-air ship which is driven by motors and propellers.

ALTIMETER. An instrument that measures how high an aircraft is above sea level at any time.

AMPHIBIAN. An airplane that can land and take off from both land and water.

AUTOGIRO. An aircraft in which rotors, big overhead propellers, are used instead of a wing, to keep the plane aloft.

AUTOPILOT. A device that flies the airplane automatically.

BALLOON. A lighter-than-air ship which has no engine to drive it.

BIPLANE. An airplane with both a top and bottom wing.

BLIMP. An airship with no rigid frame.

BOMBARDIER. The member of a military bomber crew who aims and releases the bombs.

CABIN. The enclosed part of the airplane, that carries cargo, passengers, and crew.

COCKPIT. The part of the airplane that is used for passengers and pilots. If the space is enclosed, it is usually called a cabin instead of a cockpit.

COWLING. A removable covering over some part of the airplane, usually the engine or cockpit.

ELEVATOR. A section of the airplane tail, which moves on hinges to make the plane go up or down.

ENGINE. The machine that drives the airplane's propellers or jet stream.

FLAP. A movable hinged portion of the rear of the wing, that enables the airplane to climb and fly fast or slow.

FLYING BOAT. A kind of seaplane in which the body itself serves as a boat for landing on water.

FUSELAGE. The body of the airplane, to which the wings and tail are attached.

GLIDER. A kind of airplane which soars through the air without an engine.

HELICOPTER. A kind of aircraft with big overhead propellers, called rotors, which lift the craft straight up, and also move it forward or backward.

INSTRUMENT PANEL. A board on which the plane's instruments are installed.

LANDING GEAR. The wheels and supporting structure on which the airplane lands.

MONOPLANE. An airplane with only one wing.

NACELLE. An outside structure which encloses part of the airplane, such as the engine.

ORNITHOPTER. A kind of airplane that flies by flapping its wings.

PARACHUTE. A kind of big umbrella used to slow the fall of a man or of cargo through the air.

PILOT. The man who flies an aircraft. He is also called an aviator.

PITOT TUBE. A tube with an open end which helps measure how fast a plane is going.

POD. Attached under the wing or fuselage of an airplane. It can contain a jet engine, fuel or nuclear weapon(s).

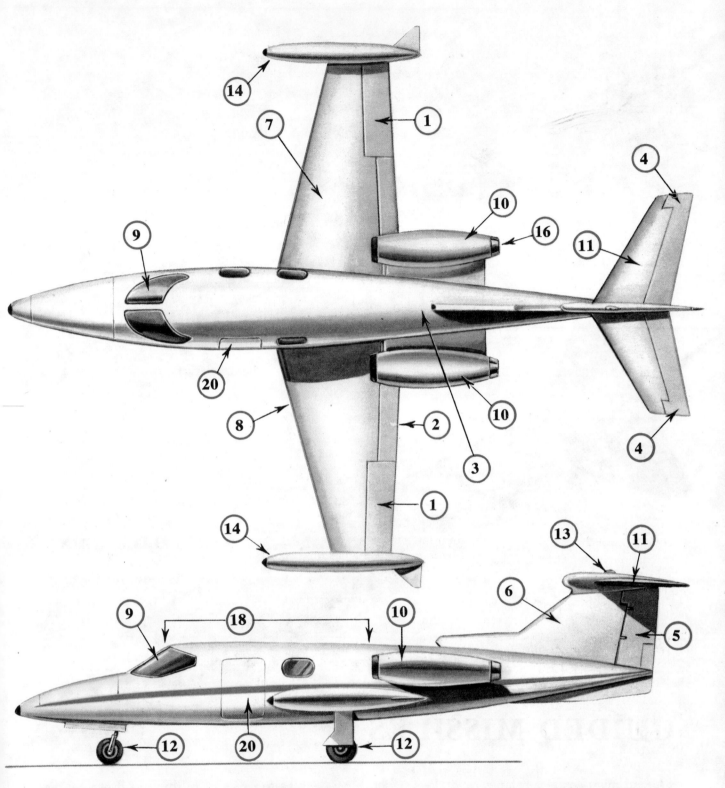

PROPELLER. A device used to push or pull a plane through the air.

RIP CORD. The rope used to open a parachute.

RUDDER. A hinged portion of the tail which helps steer the airplane from one side to the other.

SAILPLANE. A fast kind of glider.

SEAPLANE. An airplane that will land on or take off from water.

SKI. A landing gear used to land planes on snow.

SOAR. To fly without power.

STRUT. An outside support to strengthen the wing.

TABS. Hinged pieces at ends of rudder, elevator, and ailerons, which help balance the plane.

TAXI. To operate an airplane on the ground or on water.

THROTTLE. A control which regulates the speed of the engine.

TRAILING EDGE. The rear edge of a wing or propeller.

TRANSMITTER. A radio set that sends messages.

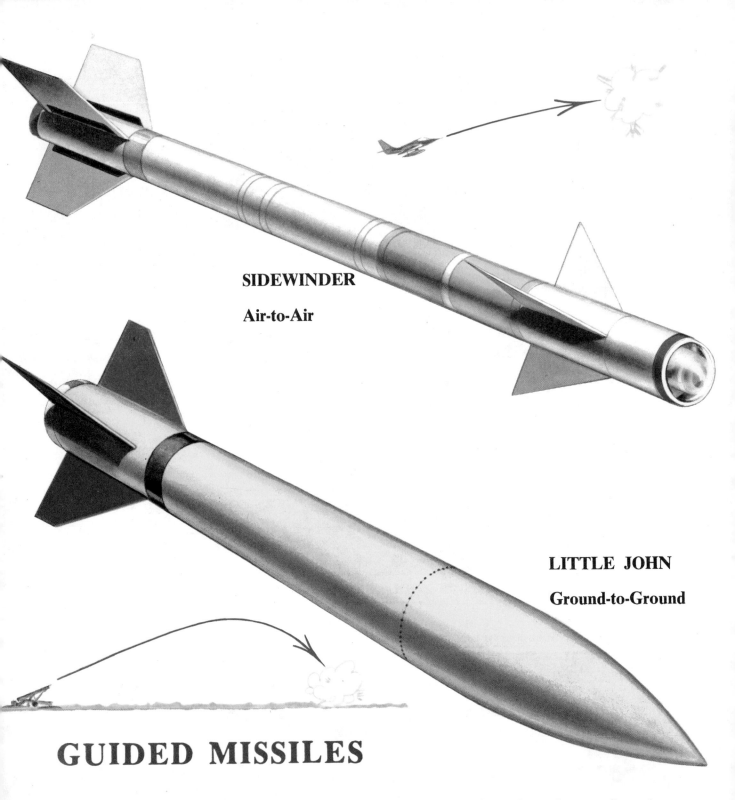

SIDEWINDER

Air-to-Air

LITTLE JOHN

Ground-to-Ground

GUIDED MISSILES

Guided missiles are airplanes or rockets which have engines to drive them, but are flown by mechanical pilots. They can be powered by liquid-fueled rocket engines, by jet engines, or by engines driving propellers. But they all have one thing in common. They are not just *aimed*, like an artillery shell or a rifle bullet. They are able to *hunt* their own targets and hit them, or else they are guided by radio or television to their targets while they are in flight. There are four types of guided missiles:

1. AIR-TO-AIR MISSILES • These are launched from airplanes and aimed at other airplanes or missiles. They can fly very fast but only for a few miles. The best air-to-air missiles are able to follow a target and hit it no matter how hard it tries to get away.

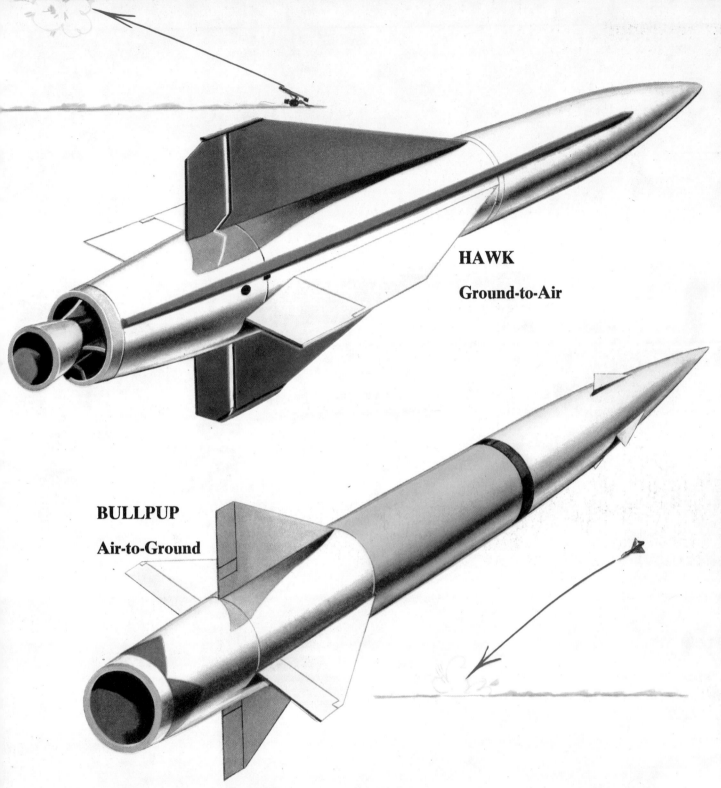

HAWK

Ground-to-Air

BULLPUP

Air-to-Ground

2. GROUND-TO-GROUND MISSILES • These are usually long-range missiles, like the German V-2 rocket. Some day, scientists believe, they may be able to hit targets 10,000 miles away. Really successful ones will not be developed for many years, however.

3. GROUND-TO-AIR MISSILES • A kind of antiaircraft weapon, they are fired from the ground to destroy enemy airplanes or enemy-guided missiles. They can be guided by radio or radar and propelled by rockets or jet engines. But they must be very fast.

4. AIR-TO-GROUND MISSILES • These are really guided bombs. Some of them automatically seek out their targets and hit them. For instance, they may have a kind of radar that is able to "smell" a steel ship or a hot factory smokestack, and fly right toward it. Such missiles may have wings and may have a rocket in the tail to make them fly faster and farther.

PAN-AMERICAN'S JET CLIPPER, BOEING 707-321B • A growing popularity and need for fast, dependable travel across oceans gave rise to the development of this great new airliner, which can carry a full load of 174 passengers between capital cities of Europe and the United States. Its range is 6,000 miles — enough to fly nonstop from Chicago to Amsterdam, Seattle to Tokyo, or New York to Rio de Janeiro. The Jet Clipper is tremendous — it has a tail fin as high as a three-story building! The wing

span alone is 145 feet 8 inches, a distance longer than that of the first flight in an airplane by the Wright Brothers. Four jet engines produce three to four times the power used to run the average ocean-going freighter. When fully loaded, the Jet Clipper weighs 325,000 pounds, yet it can fly safely on three engines and stay in the air with two engines cut off. Its cruising speed at 42,000 feet is 575 miles per hour. The Jet Clippers are flown to all six continents and on round-the-world service.

HOW ENGINES OPERATE

RECIPROCATING ENGINE

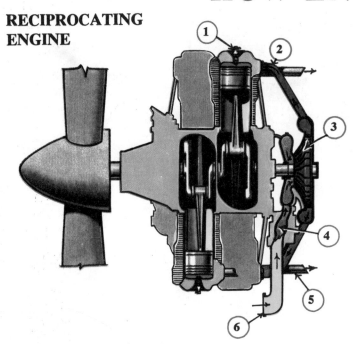

KEY TO NUMBERS

1. Spark Plug
2. Cylinder Inlet
3. Shaft-Driven Supercharger
4. Carburetor
5. Cylinder Exhaust
6. Air Scoop
7. Air Inlet
8. Propeller
9. Reduction Gear
10. Compressor
11. Fuel Spray
12. Compressor-Drive Turbine
13. Tail Cone
14. Propeller-Drive Turbine
15. Combuster
16. Turbine
17. Adjustable Exhaust Nozzle
18. Fuel
19. Oxidant
20. Pump Unit
21. Combustion Chamber
22. Exhaust Nozzle
23. Shock Wave
24. Fuel Injection
25. Flame Holder

TURBOJET

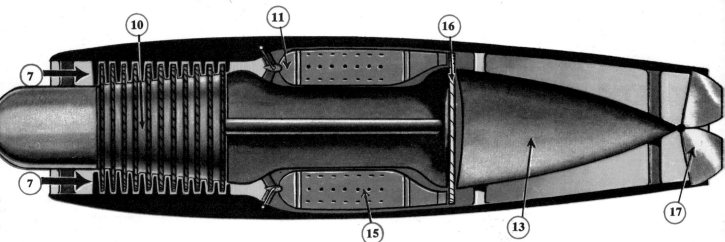

The engine that turns a propeller is called a *reciprocating* engine. Air comes into the engine through an air scoop on the outside of the plane. Then the air goes into a supercharger, where it is forced into a very small space. After that, the air is forced into a cylinder and compressed into a space even smaller. The fuel is burned in the cylinder. When the fuel burns, it causes the air to expand and take up more space. As the air expands, it pushes a piston. Then the air escapes through the cylinder exhaust. Every time a piston is pushed by the expanding air, the piston helps turn a crankshaft. And on the end of the crankshaft is the propeller, which turns rapidly. The propeller thrusts the air behind it, and causes the plane to move through the air.

Air blown into a balloon is compressed by forcing it into a smaller space inside the balloon. Then, by releasing the balloon, air spurts out of its mouth, causing the balloon to move in the opposite direction. That's how a jet engine works. In a *turbojet,* air flows into an inlet and is forced into a small space by a compressor. Fuel is sprayed and then burned in the combuster. The heat

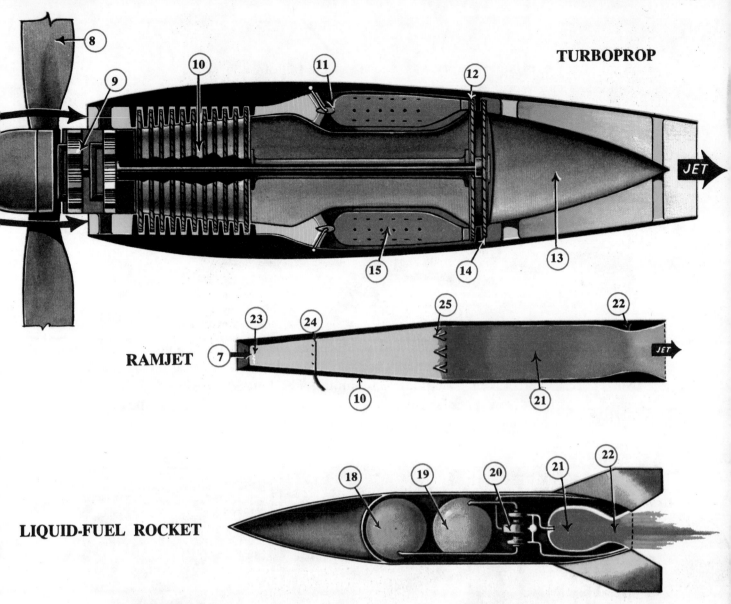

TURBOPROP

RAMJET

LIQUID-FUEL ROCKET

causes the air to expand and spurt out of an exhaust nozzle that may be adjusted to control the thrust. Just before the air escapes, it turns a turbine wheel which causes the compressor to operate, so it does an extra job, besides causing the airplane to move forward.

The *turboprop* engine has a turbine wheel, too, but in addition to operating the compressor, it is attached to a crankshaft, which turns a propeller.

One of the simplest airplane engines is the *ramjet*. It looks like a simple tube or pipe. In fact, some people call it a flying stovepipe. The air intake is narrow, shaped so that the air coming into the engine has to slow down. The air is thus compressed and forced into a small space. Then fuel is injected and burned. As the fuel burns, it heats the air, which expands, rushing out of the exhaust nozzle at a much faster speed than when it entered the air intake. The ramjet is best for fast planes, but it is also being used as a helicopter engine, with one ramjet on the tip of each rotor.

The fastest airplane engines are called rockets. They are good engines for flying at great heights and for flying very fast. But they can fly for only a short time because they burn so much fuel. A rocket engine carries its own fuel, plus oxygen needed to burn the fuel. One kind of rocket is called a *liquid-fuel rocket*. It has two tanks — one for fuel, the other for the "oxidant" which when mixed with the fuel enables it to burn without outside air. The engine usually operates with a pump unit. Very little of the liquid fuel is used to operate the pump, which mixes the oxidant and fuel. The mixture goes into the combustion chamber, where it burns at a very hot temperature, and escapes through the exhaust nozzle.

A milestone in aviation history was reached in the fall of 1955, when Pan American World Airways placed orders for the first fleet of jet airliners—45 in all—to usher in the jet air age.

Jet clippers fly high above clouds and weather, in the deep purple-blue of the substratosphere, where passengers can actually see the stars at noon! Transatlantic crossings from New York to Paris take only 6 hours 35 minutes. The longest nonstop flight Pan American schedules is from New York to Buenos Aires, a distance of 5,310 miles, lasting ten and a half hours — longer than a flight from New York to Moscow.

The day seats in the cabin section of a Jet Clipper convert into comfortable beds at night, with both upper and lower berths as large as standard single beds in your home. Imagine falling asleep six or seven miles above the world, with no sound or motion to disturb you! Even at that altitude, the controlled atmosphere within the cabin is no thinner than the air at a place such as Colorado Springs.

The gigantic Jet Clippers, costing nearly $6,000,000 each, contain a beautiful, luxurious lounge such as the one pictured, where passengers enjoy silent jet flight, comfort, security, and numerous personal services and conveniences. The fantastic speed of these Jet Clippers makes possible round-trips to Europe in a single day, as well as lower fares, thereby permitting many people who could not ordinarily afford the time or the cost an opportunity to visit other countries. Jet Clippers thus promote the cause of international peace by broadening the understanding of people of all nations as they "sky-hop" from country to country.

The flight deck of a Jet Clipper is actually simpler than the cockpit of a conventional airliner. Jet engines need no propeller controls and therefore many of the usual instruments are unnecessary.

BOEING 727 • A growing need for a jet to fill the gap in air transportation (not covered by the larger jets) to smaller cities located off the main traffic routes, as well as to provide economical through-stop service along main routes, brought about the development of the Boeing 727. Its range of 2,500 miles allows it to make many short flights without refueling. Three turbofan (fanjet) engines, each having a thrust of 14,000 pounds, are

mounted at the rear of the airplane. At an altitude of 37,000 feet, the 727's cruising speed is more than 600 miles per hour. It carries from 71 to 131 passengers. The fuselage is 137 feet 8 inches long; the tail is 34 feet high; the wing span is 108 feet. In the picture above you see a British West Indian Airways 727, which connects various islands in the Caribbean with the mainland of the United States and South America.

**Ling-Temco-Vought
L.T.V. A-7A**

**North American
A-5A VIGILANTE**

WARPLANES

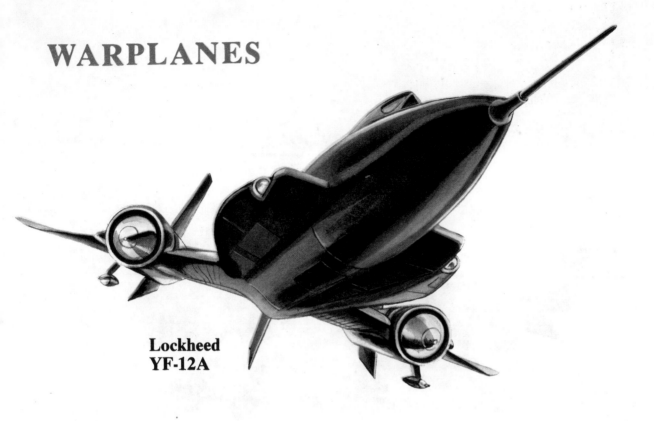

**Lockheed
YF-12A**

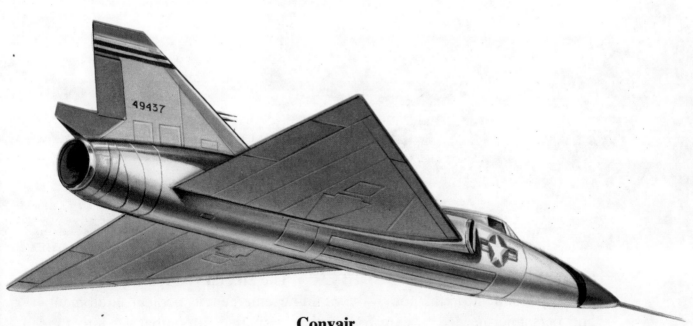

**Convair
F-106A DELTA DART**

"FLYING CRANE" HELICOPTER • The Sikorsky "Flying Crane" can carry a mobile-hospital pod — containing emergency medical equipment and personnel needed to care for soldiers wounded in combat — into the thick of battle. In the picture, it is descending to the side of a mountain on an urgent medical mission. Because of its great lifting ability, this helicopter has virtually opened up a new area of work for itself. It could carry sections of a bridge or a steel tower — or even tow a vessel in distress.

MANNED SPACE ROCKET X-15 • The performance of the X-15 keeps changing as man learns more about space flight. At the present time it is capable of reaching an altitude of 100,000 feet and flying eight times faster than the speed of sound. Under such conditions the outside surface of the craft is heated to a temperature of over 2,400° F. In practice, a B-52 plane (known here as the mother-ship) takes the X-15 to an altitude of about 45,000 feet. The rocket engines are then started, whereupon the X-15 separates from the mother-ship and flies off into space. The yellow tank pod on its side contains extra fuel for longer flights.

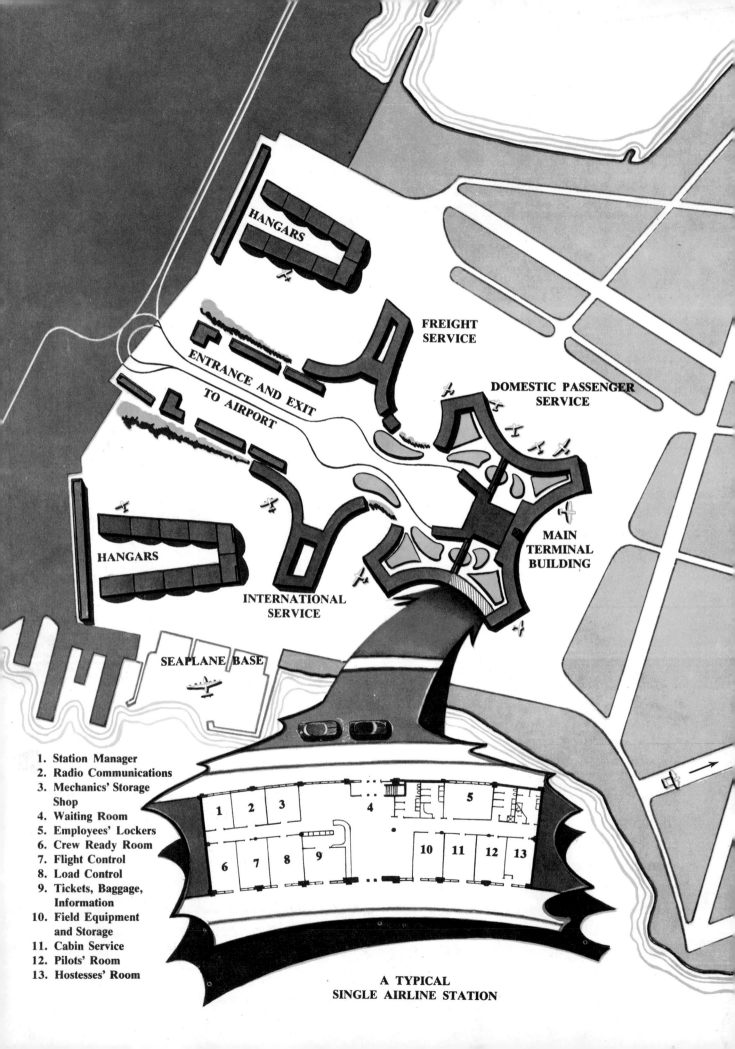

HANGARS

FREIGHT
SERVICE

ENTRANCE AND EXIT

TO AIRPORT

DOMESTIC PASSENGER
SERVICE

HANGARS

INTERNATIONAL
SERVICE

MAIN
TERMINAL
BUILDING

SEAPLANE BASE

1. Station Manager
2. Radio Communications
3. Mechanics' Storage
   Shop
4. Waiting Room
5. Employees' Lockers
6. Crew Ready Room
7. Flight Control
8. Load Control
9. Tickets, Baggage,
   Information
10. Field Equipment
    and Storage
11. Cabin Service
12. Pilots' Room
13. Hostesses' Room

A TYPICAL
SINGLE AIRLINE STATION

HOW AN AIRPORT OPERATES

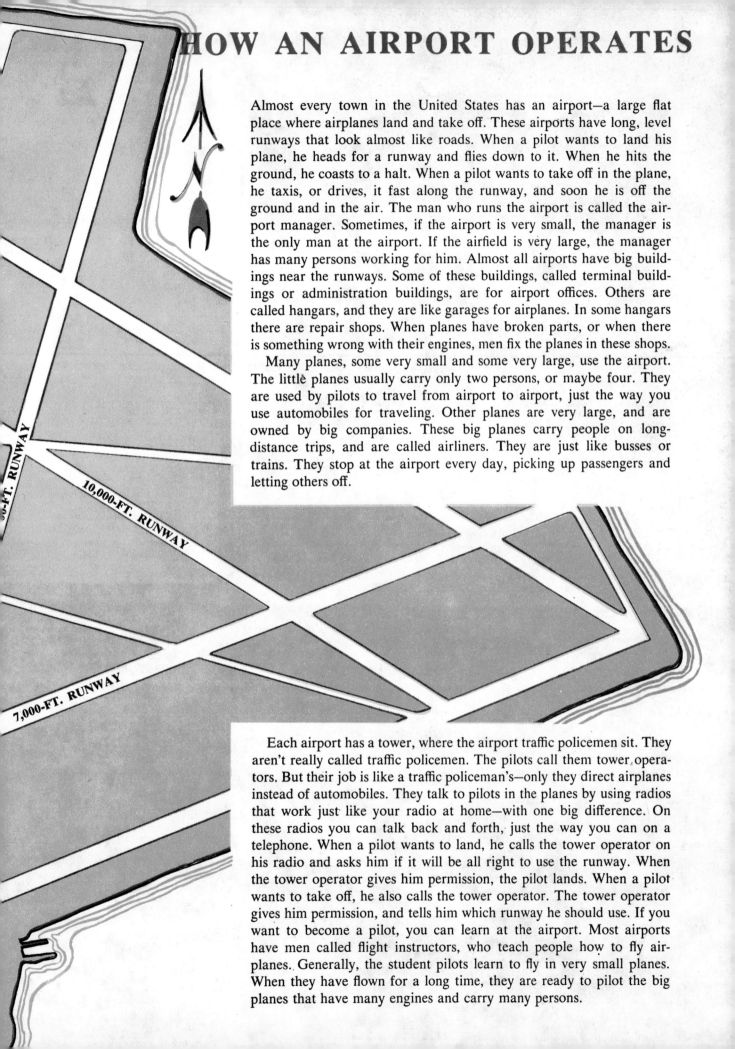

10,000-FT. RUNWAY

7,000-FT. RUNWAY

Almost every town in the United States has an airport—a large flat place where airplanes land and take off. These airports have long, level runways that look almost like roads. When a pilot wants to land his plane, he heads for a runway and flies down to it. When he hits the ground, he coasts to a halt. When a pilot wants to take off in the plane, he taxis, or drives, it fast along the runway, and soon he is off the ground and in the air. The man who runs the airport is called the airport manager. Sometimes, if the airport is very small, the manager is the only man at the airport. If the airfield is very large, the manager has many persons working for him. Almost all airports have big buildings near the runways. Some of these buildings, called terminal buildings or administration buildings, are for airport offices. Others are called hangars, and they are like garages for airplanes. In some hangars there are repair shops. When planes have broken parts, or when there is something wrong with their engines, men fix the planes in these shops.

Many planes, some very small and some very large, use the airport. The little planes usually carry only two persons, or maybe four. They are used by pilots to travel from airport to airport, just the way you use automobiles for traveling. Other planes are very large, and are owned by big companies. These big planes carry people on long-distance trips, and are called airliners. They are just like busses or trains. They stop at the airport every day, picking up passengers and letting others off.

Each airport has a tower, where the airport traffic policemen sit. They aren't really called traffic policemen. The pilots call them tower operators. But their job is like a traffic policeman's—only they direct airplanes instead of automobiles. They talk to pilots in the planes by using radios that work just like your radio at home—with one big difference. On these radios you can talk back and forth, just the way you can on a telephone. When a pilot wants to land, he calls the tower operator on his radio and asks him if it will be all right to use the runway. When the tower operator gives him permission, the pilot lands. When a pilot wants to take off, he also calls the tower operator. The tower operator gives him permission, and tells him which runway he should use. If you want to become a pilot, you can learn at the airport. Most airports have men called flight instructors, who teach people how to fly airplanes. Generally, the student pilots learn to fly in very small planes. When they have flown for a long time, they are ready to pilot the big planes that have many engines and carry many persons.

GOOSENECK TRAILER • The gooseneck trailer carries heavy machinery and steam shovels. Sometimes it even carries houses.

Do you see the front of the trailer? It goes over the wheels of the tractor. It is like the neck of a goose.

The gooseneck trailer and tractor has 14 wheels. It has 8 wheels on the trailer. It has 6 wheels on the tractor.

The driver works the brakes of the trailer. He works them from the seat of the cab. He works the lights, too.

TANK TRAILER • This truck carries gasoline. It is carried in the big tank behind the tractor. The inside of the big tank is divided into sections. This keeps the gasoline from going to one side of the truck. An even load makes it easier for the man to drive the truck.

Gasoline trucks have a chain dragging on the road. This chain sends electricity from the truck into the ground. The chain keeps sparks from setting fire to the gasoline. The word "Gasolene" on the truck is a trade name. Do you see the difference in the spelling?

EUCLID DUMP TRUCK • This dump truck can carry tons of earth or rock over very rough ground. It is used on many road-building jobs. The tires have a deep tread, like snow tires, which helps the truck move more easily in mud or soft earth.

The truck moves by Diesel power. Heavy smoke from the Diesel
engine comes out of the two tall pipes above the hood, in front.

The wire blanket is used to cover rock when blasting. It protects
workmen from being hit by small flying rocks.

SCENICRUISER • This streamlined bus is higher and longer than most buses. Passengers look out of the big windows. They get a good view as the bus goes along. The passengers sit on two different levels. The luggage is kept in the bottom of the bus.

The bus is air-conditioned. It is heated in cold weather. The bus rides smoothly. The seats are comfortable.

On long trips the bus stops at stations along the way. Passengers may then get out and walk around. They may get something to eat.

LOW-BED TRAILER • This special tractor-trailer is needed when a very heavy transformer, such as the one shown above, is moved. The jeep-dolly trailer in front of the low-bed trailer helps spread the weight of the load on the ground. There are fifty tires in all.

The travel route of such a trailer is always checked ahead of time for clearance, such as at turns and underpasses. A small truck leads the way and another small truck follows behind. The Diesel engine in the tractor up front uses about five gallons of fuel per mile.

1. The truck driver gets up late in the morning. He dresses and has his breakfast. Then he goes to work. He is ready to start the day.

2. He checks in. He finds which truck he is to drive. He gets his log book. He must write about his trip in the log book.

5. The truck driver stops at a toll gate. He has to pay a toll to go through. Trucks often have to pay more than passenger cars.

6. The truck driver stops to eat. He writes the time in his log book. A driver must not drive more than ten hours. This is a law.

9. If a truck stops on a road, the driver uses flare pots. These are long-burning oil lamps. The flare pots warn other cars. The driver writes the time of his stop in his log book.

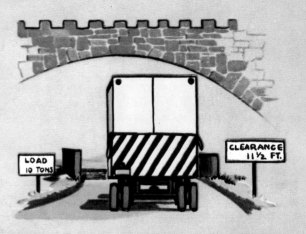

3. Men have greased and oiled the truck. They have filled it with gasoline. They have checked the motors. The truck is ready to go.

4. The truck driver is given a route to follow. The heavy truck travels only over strong roads and bridges. It can go only under high bridges.

7. State laws tell how much weight trucks may carry in order to go on certain roads. Drivers must stop at weighing stations.

8. The driver goes fast along a straight road where there is little traffic. He goes slower when there is heavy traffic on the road.

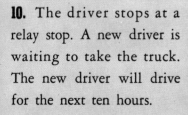

10. The driver stops at a relay stop. A new driver is waiting to take the truck. The new driver will drive for the next ten hours.

The driver goes to a hotel to sleep. The next morning he goes to the relay stop. He drives another truck back to his home.

REFRIGERATOR TRAILER • The inside of this trailer is kept cold by its own Diesel-powered refrigerator. Butter, eggs, meat, fish, fruit and vegetables are kept fresh as the food is sent to places hundreds of miles away. The trailer can also carry frozen foods.

A Diesel tractor pulls the trailer. See the tall exhaust pipe just behind the cab? Sometimes trucks travel very far with two drivers. The cab of the tractor in this picture has a bed just behind the driver's seat. One of the men can sleep while the other one drives.

DIESEL FREIGHT TRAILER • This trailer carries many things. Often these things, called freight, are taken to stores in another state. Freight trucks are big. They have many different state license plates on them.

The front part of the truck is called the tractor. This has the cab and the motor. The back part is called the trailer. This truck has a Diesel motor. This motor is cheaper to run than a gasoline motor.

MOVING VAN TRAILER   •   Trailers such as this one are used to move furniture and household things to a new home or apartment. Small things and clothes are carefully packed in boxes and sealed. Furniture is covered with a blanket before something else is put on top.

Because the wheels at the back end of the trailer are smaller than the ones up front, there is more loading space inside the van. The men load the trailer so that everything inside is snug. If this is not done, things might get damaged from bumping about.

WHAT MAKES AN ENGINE RUN?

PARTS OF A V-8 ENGINE

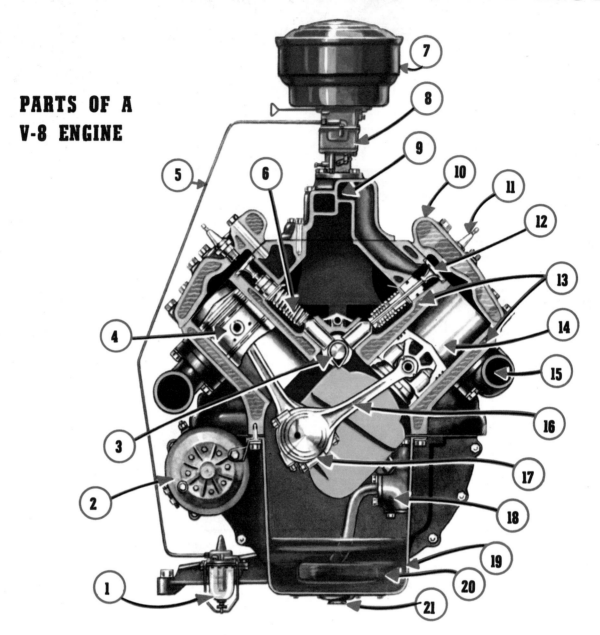

1 Fuel Pump	9 Intake Manifold	17 Crankshaft with Connecting Rod Attached
2 Starter	10 Cylinder Head	
3 Camshaft	11 Spark Plug	
4 Four-Ring Piston	12 Valve	18 Oil Pump
5 Fuel Line	13 Water Jacket	19 Crankcase
6 Valve Spring	14 Cylinder Wall	20 Oil
7 Air Filter	15 Exhaust Manifold	21 Drain Plug
8 Carburetor	16 Connecting Rod	

Can you ride a bicycle? You make it go by using your legs. They give power to the pedals. A gasoline engine runs the same way. The piston action on the crankshaft is the same as your feet pressing on the bicycle pedals.

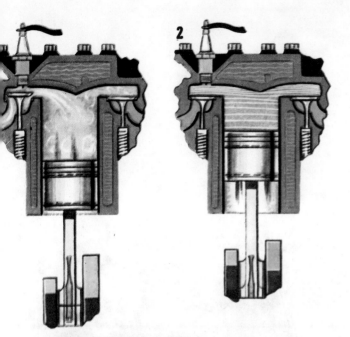
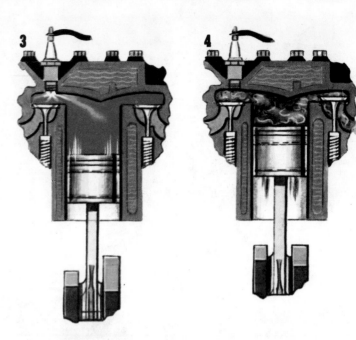

A COMPLETE POWER CYCLE • There are four strokes in a complete power cycle.

1. INTAKE STROKE • This is stroke one. It goes down. The starter turns the crankshaft. The piston takes gas vapor through the intake valve on the left.

2. COMPRESSION STROKE • This is stroke two. It goes up. The intake valve on the left closes. Then the piston starts going up. When the piston goes up, it compresses the gas vapor.

3. POWER STROKE • This is stroke three. It goes down. The spark plug is timed by the distributor. The spark ignites the compressed gas vapor. The explosion makes the piston go down. This makes the crankshaft go around.

4. EXHAUST STROKE • This is stroke four. It goes up. The burned gas vapors are pushed out of the valve to the right. The valve closes. This completes the cycle.

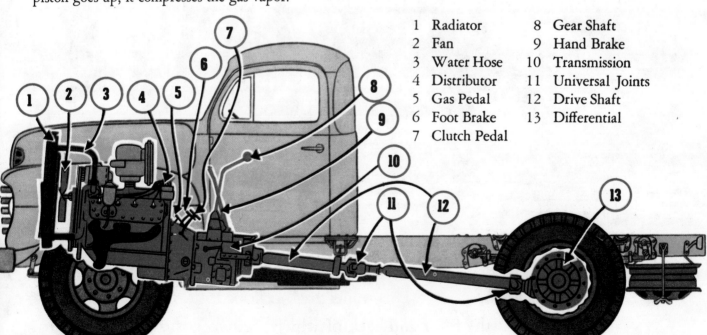
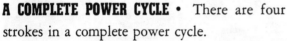

1	Radiator	8	Gear Shaft
2	Fan	9	Hand Brake
3	Water Hose	10	Transmission
4	Distributor	11	Universal Joints
5	Gas Pedal	12	Drive Shaft
6	Foot Brake	13	Differential
7	Clutch Pedal		

This is how the engine makes the truck run. First the driver starts the engine. Then the driver steps on the gas pedal.

The engine starts turning the drive shaft. The drive shaft turns the gears. This turns the rear wheels. Now the truck moves.

LUMBER TRAILER • This trailer has no floor to it. It has a long center beam, at the front and back of which are two U-shaped pieces holding the bottom logs on the trailer. Chains are placed around all of the logs when there is a full load. Then the chains are locked.

This type of trailer can also carry steel girders, metal pipes, or concrete pipes.

In this picture, the logs are being taken to a sawmill where they will be cut into boards.

AIRPORT FIRE TRUCK • The airport fire truck has a big water tank. It uses water from a hydrant, too. The truck goes to any part of the airport to put out a fire. The truck has a tank of foam. The foam is used to keep gasoline and hot metal parts from catching fire.

The turret gun is used to shoot either water or foam. The hose on the reel shoots foam in a spray.

The airport fire truck is an emergency truck. The fire truck also carries first-aid equipment.

AIRPORT REFUELER • This truck is like a gas station on wheels. It is used to refuel jets at airports. It holds 8,000 gallons of fuel.

There is a double set of wheels in front. First, there are two tires, one on each side. Then there are four tires, two on each side. When

the driver turns his steering wheel, all six of these tires turn. Usually a regular tractor-trailer would be needed for such a heavy load, but a trailer is hard to back up. The airport refueler is all one truck. It carries a heavy load, and it is easily moved into place.

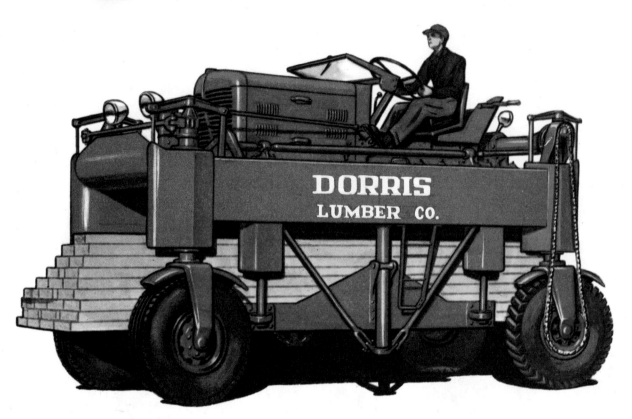

STRADDLE LUMBER TRUCK • This truck stands over, or straddles, a pile of lumber. It loads the lumber from underneath. The lumber is piled on a low platform.

The driver moves the truck over the pile. He pulls a lever. One long arm drops down on each side of the platform. These arms lift the lumber. The arms hold the lumber in place.

FLUSHING MACHINE • This truck moves along in the middle of the street. Water comes from faucets on both sides of the truck.

The water cleans the street. In warm weather, the flushing machine is sometimes used to cool the hot pavements.

HEAVY DUMP TRUCK • This truck carries big rocks. It is made of steel. It has strong braces. The front edge of the body covers the cab. This protects the cab from falling rocks.

Pumps make the body of the truck go up and down. Some dump trucks are very heavy. They cannot go on regular roads. Their heavy weight would crack the pavement.

ELGIN SWEEPER • This truck has brooms that clean the streets. It takes the place of men.

This truck can clean most places. The places that the truck cannot reach are swept by hand.

FLAT-BED TRAILER • There are no sides or back to this trailer. It has a wall at the front end to protect the driver from shifting cargo, caused by sudden stops. The cargo of rough-cut maple boards in this picture is separated into sections for easier loading and unloading.

The flat-bed trailer is used for hauling small machines such as
farm tractors, small cement mixers and water pumps. It also carries
concrete blocks, cut stone and wooden crates.

CONCRETE MIXER • This truck delivers concrete. It mixes the concrete while the truck is going along the road. The mixer tank is filled with sand, cement, and gravel. The mixer tank mixes them together. The mixer tank is turned by a motor.

The water tank is behind the cab. Water is run into the mixer from the water tank. It mixes with sand, cement, and gravel.

When the truck arrives at the job, the concrete is ready to be used. The driver opens the mixer. The concrete pours down the chute.

CEMENT TANK-TRAILER • This trailer is being backed up onto the scale at the cement plant. The rear wheels are put on the scale first and weighed. Then the rear tractor wheels are weighed. The tank is then filled with dry cement and another weighing takes place.

An air-compressor on the back of the trailer is used to unload the dry cement by air pressure. The pipe at the lower center of the tank-trailer is connected to a receiving line for unloading the dry cement wherever it is needed.

LIVESTOCK TRUCK • The livestock truck is used to carry cattle from farms and ranches to the market. On large ranches it carries cattle to the mountains in the spring. It brings them back to the low, warm valleys in the winter.

The sides have open spaces. There is a roof over the trailer to protect the cattle. A gate in the back opens for loading and unloading. When cattle are unloaded, the truck is backed up to a platform. The animals walk off the truck onto the platform.

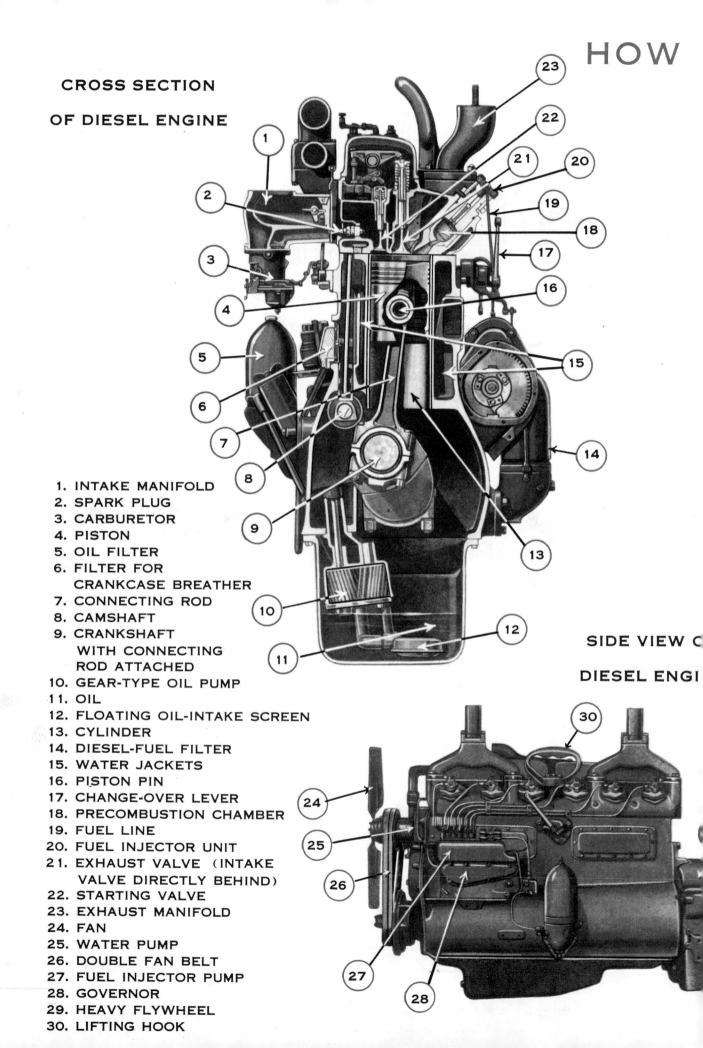

CROSS SECTION

OF DIESEL ENGINE

SIDE VIEW C

DIESEL ENGI

1. INTAKE MANIFOLD
2. SPARK PLUG
3. CARBURETOR
4. PISTON
5. OIL FILTER
6. FILTER FOR
   CRANKCASE BREATHER
7. CONNECTING ROD
8. CAMSHAFT
9. CRANKSHAFT
   WITH CONNECTING
   ROD ATTACHED
10. GEAR-TYPE OIL PUMP
11. OIL
12. FLOATING OIL-INTAKE SCREEN
13. CYLINDER
14. DIESEL-FUEL FILTER
15. WATER JACKETS
16. PISTON PIN
17. CHANGE-OVER LEVER
18. PRECOMBUSTION CHAMBER
19. FUEL LINE
20. FUEL INJECTOR UNIT
21. EXHAUST VALVE (INTAKE
    VALVE DIRECTLY BEHIND)
22. STARTING VALVE
23. EXHAUST MANIFOLD
24. FAN
25. WATER PUMP
26. DOUBLE FAN BELT
27. FUEL INJECTOR PUMP
28. GOVERNOR
29. HEAVY FLYWHEEL
30. LIFTING HOOK

DIESEL ENGINE RUNS

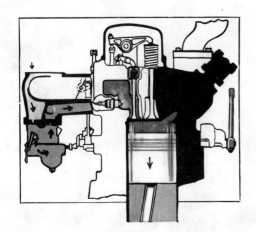

A Diesel operates on oil fired not by a spark, but by compression heat. Therefore, a cold Diesel must be started by some other power source in order to warm up the engine for Diesel fuel. Here, it is started with gasoline in the auxiliary combustion chamber (shown in black in pictures 1, 2, 3, and 4). With the change-over lever in "start" position, the Diesel part (shown in black in picture at left) is not working. After a minute, the change-over switches the engine to Diesel operation and the gasoline part stops working.

A DIESEL POWER CYCLE

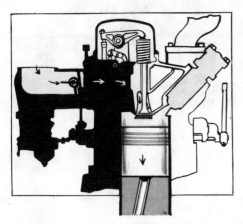

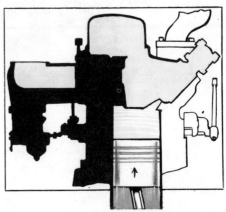

1. INTAKE STROKE • The intake valve opens and the piston goes down. In this view the intake valve (with head shown in red) is located directly behind the exhaust valve. On the intake stroke a Diesel sucks in air, alone (shown in blue, above), unlike a gasoline engine, which draws in a fuel-air mixture.

2. COMPRESSION STROKE • Now all valves are closed and the piston rises, greatly compressing the air inside. The temperature of the air charge is suddenly boosted.

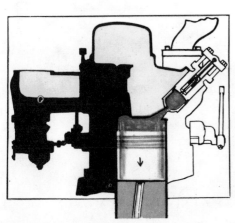

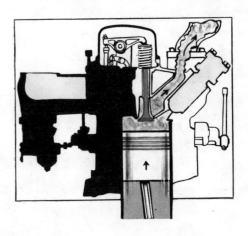

3. POWER STROKE • As the piston nears top dead center, oil is injected in a spray and is ignited by compression heat. This forces the piston down, giving power to the crankshaft.

4. EXHAUST STROKE • The exhaust valve (here shown in red) opens and the piston starts its last upstroke of the cycle, forcing the burned gases into the exhaust manifold. At the top of its stroke, the piston begins the cycle again.

SNOW PLOWS • Snow plows are used in places where the snow falls. The plow is put on the front of the truck. It can be put up or down. After the road is scraped, the snow plow is taken off.

The truck is loaded with snow. It is dumped in a river or on an empty lot. The truck also carries sand. The road men throw sand on the icy roads. This keeps the cars from skidding.

TRAINS

THE LOCOMOTIVE AND TENDER · The engine comes out of the roundhouse. It is cleaned and oiled. The tender behind the engine carries coal and water. The locomotive is ready for a trip. This locomotive has four pilot

wheels in front. These keep the engine on a track. It has six driving wheels. These make the engine go. Four other wheels carry the back of the engine.

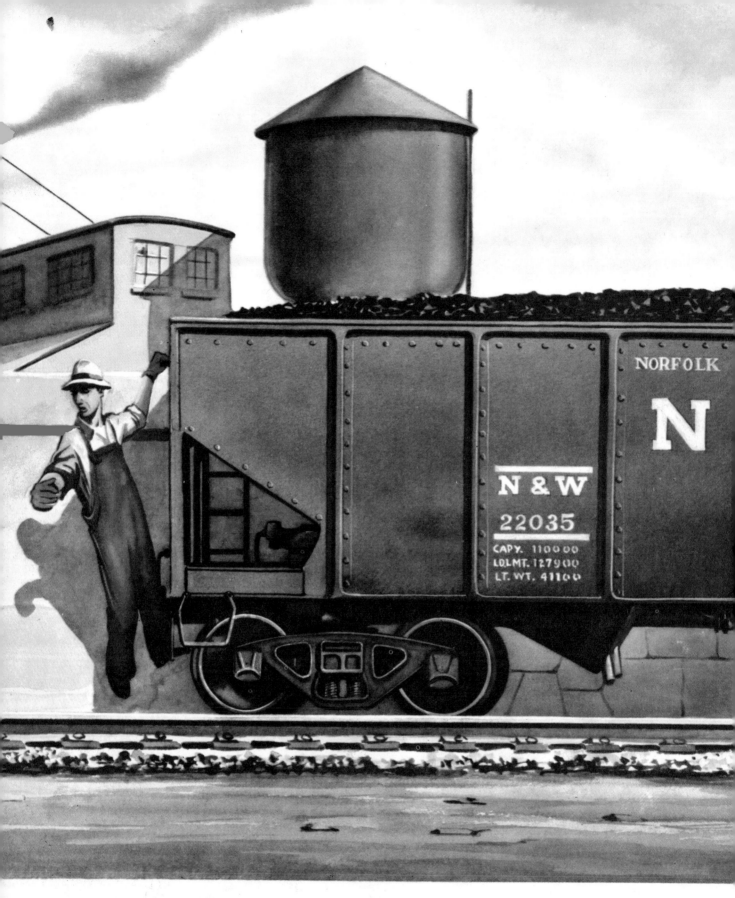

HOPPER • A steel hopper car carries coal and gravel. It also carries different kinds of ore. A hopper is loaded from the top. It is loaded by an auto-

matic loader. A switch engine moves the hopper under the loading bin. The coal or gravel goes through the chutes into the hopper.

COVERED HOPPER · The covered hopper has a roof over the top. There are eight hatches on the roof. The hatches are opened to load the

hopper. The covered hopper carries sugar, cement or grain. No moisture can
get in to harden the hopper's cargo.

FLAT CAR · A flat car is a platform on wheels. It has no top or walls. It has stakes instead along the sides. The stakes keep the cargo in the flat car from falling off. Flat cars can haul large pieces of machinery. They also haul

huge logs and boards from the sawmills. Sometimes big tractors are carried on a flat car.

SUPER FLAT CAR · The super flat car has thirty-two wheels. The center of the super flat car is depressed. Huge heavy machinery or electric

transformers are carried in the depressed center. The center is depressed so that the car can go under bridges with its cargo.

CATTLE CAR • This livestock car carries cattle. It has one deck. It has slits
on each side to let in fresh air for the animals. Some livestock cars carry sheep
and pigs. They have two decks. Cars that carry chickens and turkeys have

many decks. Animals cannot travel more than a day and a half in a freight car. This is the law. The cattle cars stop at resting places. The animals have food and water in the resting pens. They have time to exercise, too.

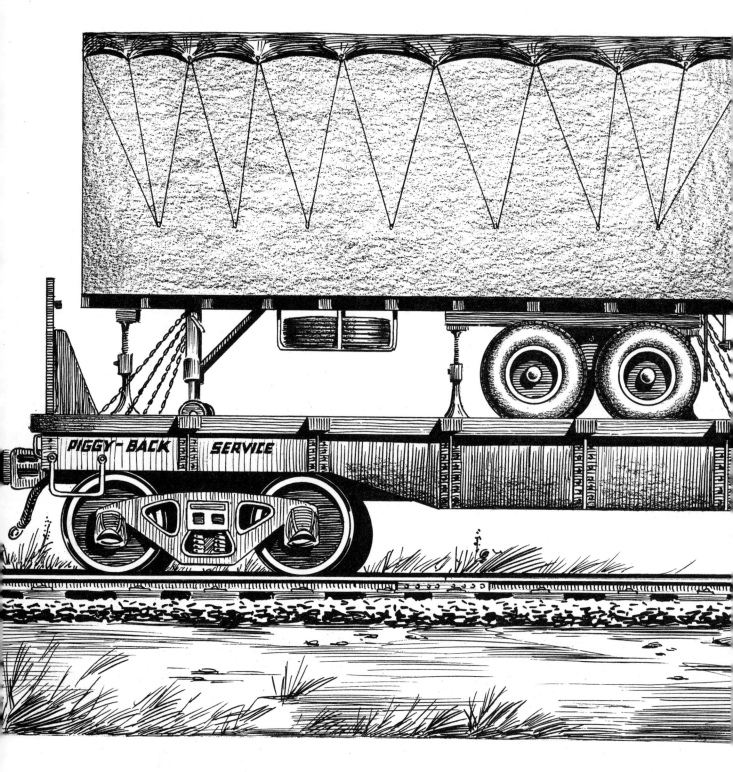

PIGGY-BACK CAR · The piggy-back car carries trailer boxes. Some piggy-back cars carry one trailer box. Others carry two. Some trains are made up only of piggy-back cars. These trains travel mostly at night. The

trailer box is secured to the deck of the piggy-back car. Jacks are placed under the box. The jacks hold the body of the trailer box up, in case the box gets a flat tire.

THE GONDOLA · The gondola is a metal box on wheels. It has no top. It carries things that snow and rain cannot hurt. It is loaded and unloaded by men. Sometimes the men use machines to load the car.

Gondolas haul pieces of machinery. They haul pipes, cement blocks, steel plates and other things.

AUTO CAR · The auto car carries new cars from the factory. It carries them to all parts of the country. Each auto car carries nine standard-size

cars. The auto car can carry fifteen compact cars. Automobiles ride safely in the auto car.

Text visible on the railroad car:

A.R.T.
22818

MAX. WT ON RAIL 136
LOAD LIMIT 74
LIGHT WT. 61

Text on the building: A. MATHEWSON INC

THE REFRIGERATOR CAR · A refrigerator car carries fruits and vegetables. It carries meat and fish. It carries butter and eggs. It even carries fresh flowers.

Men fit canvas funnels over the doors. Machines blow cold air into the car. Then the car is loaded. The doors are closed. Ice is put in at each end of the refrigerator car. More ice is put in at stations along the way.

MECHANICAL TEMPERATURE CONTROLLED CAR

Santa Fe

SFRD

2213

CAPY. 124 000 RP
LD. LMT. 124 000
LT. WT. 86 000

DIESEL FUEL No.1

MECHANICAL REFRIGERATOR CAR · The mechanical refrigerator car carries its own refrigerator. The refrigerator is run by diesel fuel. The temperature in the car can be kept at 70°, or as low as 10° below

Ship and Travel
SANTA FE
—all the way

EXW 11-2   H 11-10
EW   8-7   H 14-1
IL   44-7
IW   9-2
IH   11-7
CU.FT. 3721

Zaffo

zero. A mechanical refrigerator car carries fresh fruits and vegetables. It can also carry frozen foods.

S.C.C.X 151

CAPY. 100000 LBS.
LT. WT. 44700

SHEL

TANK CAR · Tank cars are really big cans with different kinds of linings. Milk tank cars have glass or steel linings. Cars that carry chemicals are lined with rubber, lead or aluminum. Tank cars have one or more

A.R.A. SPEC.
SAFETY VALVES
TESTED 8-40
PRESSURE 25 LBS
TANK TESTED 8-40

NEW 3-38

domes on top. In warm weather the liquid expands and goes up in the dome. If the liquid could not expand, the car might break at the seams. There are more than 200 different kinds of tank cars.

DOUBLE-DOOR BOX CAR · The double-door on the box car makes it easy to load and unload large cargo. The box car carries dry goods that are packed in boxes. It carries barrels and bales. It carries bundles and bags.

ROUTE OF THE
VISTA-DOME
NORTH COAST
LIMITED

NORTHERN PACIFIC
RAILWAY

EXW 16-7
EW 9-5
IL 40-6
IW. 9-2
IH 10-6
CU. FT. 3727

It even carries small boats. The box car is made of metal in the outside and
lined with wood on the inside.

CABOOSE • The caboose is the last car of the train. It is an office, a bedroom, and a kitchen. The rear brakeman sits in the place on top and watches the whole train. On long trips the train crew cooks dinner in the caboose.

The caboose has a telephone. The crew can talk to the engineer and the fireman up front.

CLASSIFICATION YARD · The classification yard is where you can see all kinds of freight cars. New trains are made up at one end of the yard. Incoming trains are "cut" at the classification yard. Cars that are to remain at this yard for unloading or loading are put on certain tracks. Cars that are to go on to the next terminal are put on other tracks. The train that is

being cut is at the highest point of the yard. This is called the "hump." As each car (or group of cars) is cut, it coasts downhill. Men in the two towers control the retarders. These retarders act as brakes on the coasting cars. The cars are made to slow up just enough so that they won't bang into the parked cars on the track that they are approaching.

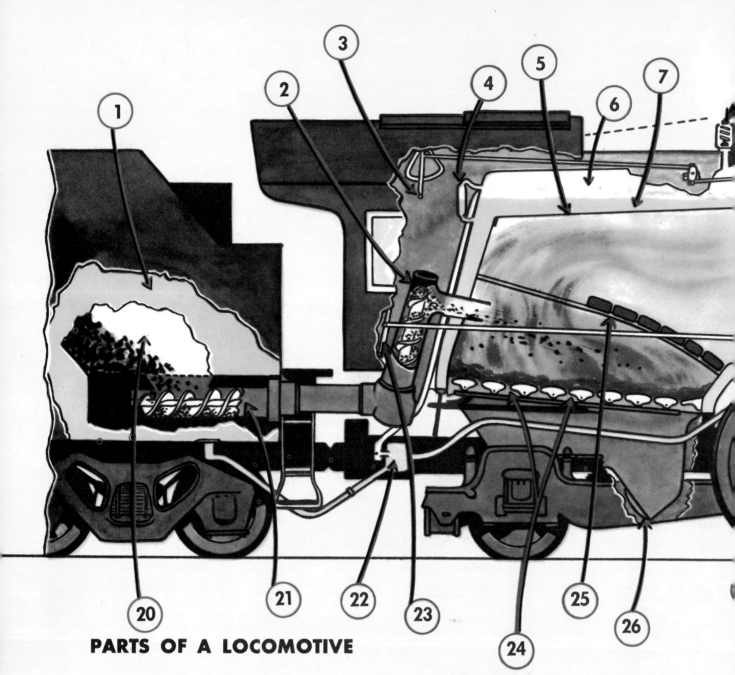

PARTS OF A LOCOMOTIVE

1 Water Tank.

2 Stoker. Coal is carried to the stoker. Steam jets blow it to all parts of the fire bed.

3 Throttle Lever.

4 Water Gauge. It shows how much water is in the boiler. Water must always cover the crown sheet. (See 5.)

5 Crown Sheet. Moist steam is blown over the crown sheet. This is the hottest part of the firebox.

6 Steam.

7 Water.

8 Safety Valve. It opens to keep the steam pressure from getting too high.

9 Throttle Valve. It controls steam that runs the locomotive.

10 Dry Pipe. It carries steam to the valve and cylinders. (See 18 and 19.)

11 Bell. It rings by air pressure.

12 Water Delivery Pipe. (See 22.)

13 Sand Dome. Sand is blown down the sand pipes if the track is slippery. (See 14.)

14 Sand Pipe.

15 Superheater Tubes.

16 Smokebox. It is filled with exhaust gases.

17 Valve Piston. It guides steam in and out of the cylinder.

18 Valve.

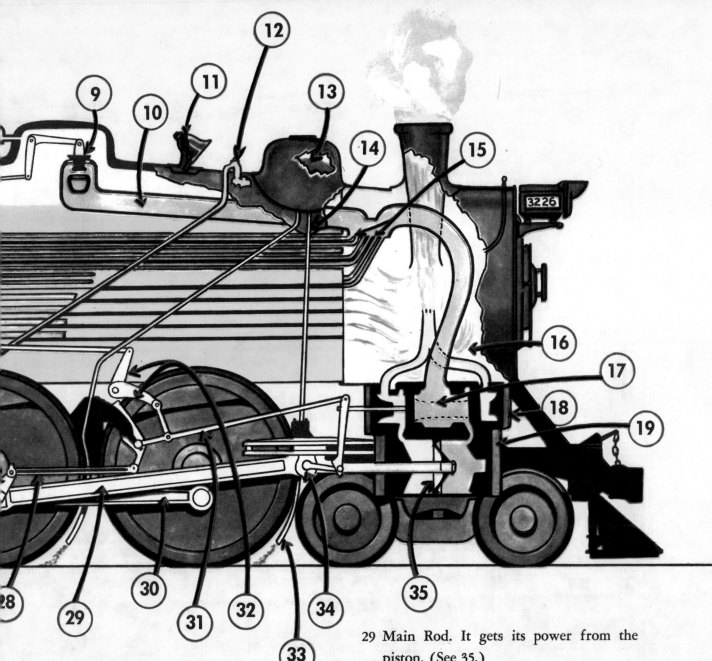

19 Cylinder.

20 Coal Bunker.

21 Worm Coal Conveyer.

22 Injector. Water comes from the tender to the injector. It mixes with a jet of steam. The steam and water push their way up the delivery pipe and into the boiler.

23 Reverse Lever.

24 Grate.

25 Brick Arch.

26 Ashpan Hopper. It lets out ashes from the grate. (See 24.)

27 Eccentric Crank.

28 Eccentric Rod.

29 Main Rod. It gets its power from the piston. (See 35.)

30 Side Rod. It takes power from the main rod to both large wheels.

31 Radius Rod. It controls the engine going forward and going backward. The radius rod is lifted up when the engine goes the other way.

32 Valve Gear. It controls the going-up or going-down of the radius rod.

33 Sand Pipe Outlet.

34 Crosshead. It is the place where the main rod joins the piston.

35 Piston. Steam comes in from the right through the dry pipe and pushes the piston to the left. This pushes the main rod and makes the engine go.

DIESEL SWITCHER · The diesel switch engine is the work horse of the yard. It is used to push or pull the many freight cars in the yard. The switch engine is used to make up a new train. It is used to move new cars to different sidings in the yard.

This diesel switch engine has the power to pull about forty-five freight cars. Railroad men call the switch engine a "drill" engine.

 # TRAIN

WHISTLE SIGNALS

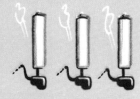

A SERIES OF SHORT TOOTS
Alarm for persons or
animals on track.

3 SHORT TOOTS
A. Back up (when train is still).
B. Stop at next station (when running).

1 SHORT TOOT
Stop.

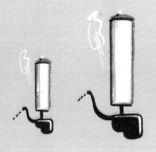

1 SHORT — 1 LONG TOOT
Brakes sticking, or inspect
train line for leak

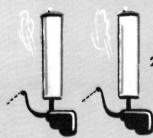

2 LONG TOOTS
Release brakes
and go ahead.

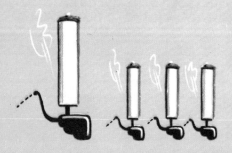

1 LONG — 3 SHORT TOOTS
Flagman, guard
rear of train.

1 LONG TOOT
Approaching station,
rail crossing, or tunnel.

AIR SIGNAL CORD

2 PULLS ON CORD
A. Start (when train is still).
B. Stop at once (when running).

3 PULLS ON CORD
A. Back train (when still).
B. Stop at next passenger station
(when running).

SIGNALS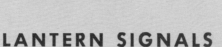

LANTERN SIGNALS

STOP

Swing back and forth across track

REDUCE SPEED

Held at arm's length

PROCEED

Raised and lowered

TRAIN PARTED

Swing in circle at arm's length across tracks

APPLY AIR BRAKES

Swing above head

RELEASE AIR BRAKES

Held at arm's length above the head

EMERGENCY STOP SIGNALS

WHAT MAKES A STREA

This is Unit "A" of a two-unit locomotive. Unit "A" co⟨n⟩-
tains the cab where the engineer and the fireman

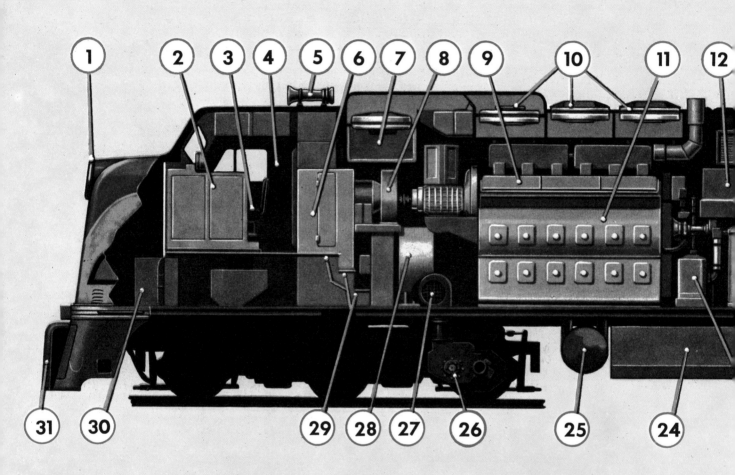

KEY TO NUMBERS

1. Headlight
2. Control Unit
3. Engineer's Seat
4. Cab
5. Horn
6. Electrical Cabinets
7. Ventilation Hatch
8. Traction Motor Blower
9. Fuel Injectors

10. Cooling System (A.C. Motor-Driv⟨e⟩
    Fans)
11. 12-Cylinder Diesel Engine (1125 h.p⟨.⟩
    There are two engines in this un⟨it⟩
    making a total of 2250 h.p.
12. Oil Cooler
13. Dynamic Brakes
14. Outer Shell of Locomotive. The oth⟨er⟩
    1125-h.p. engine is inside.

. Separate Steam Generator Room

. Coupler

. Toilet

. Brake Cylinder

. Springs

. Brake Shoes

. Sand Pipe

. Main Air Reservoirs

. Water-Cooled Air Compressor

24. Combination Fuel and Water Tank
   1200 gals. of fuel, 1350 gals. of water

25. Main Air Reservoirs

26. Traction Motor

27. Blower, for Traction Motor

28. Main Generator

29. Steps

30. Air-Brake Equipment

31. Pilot

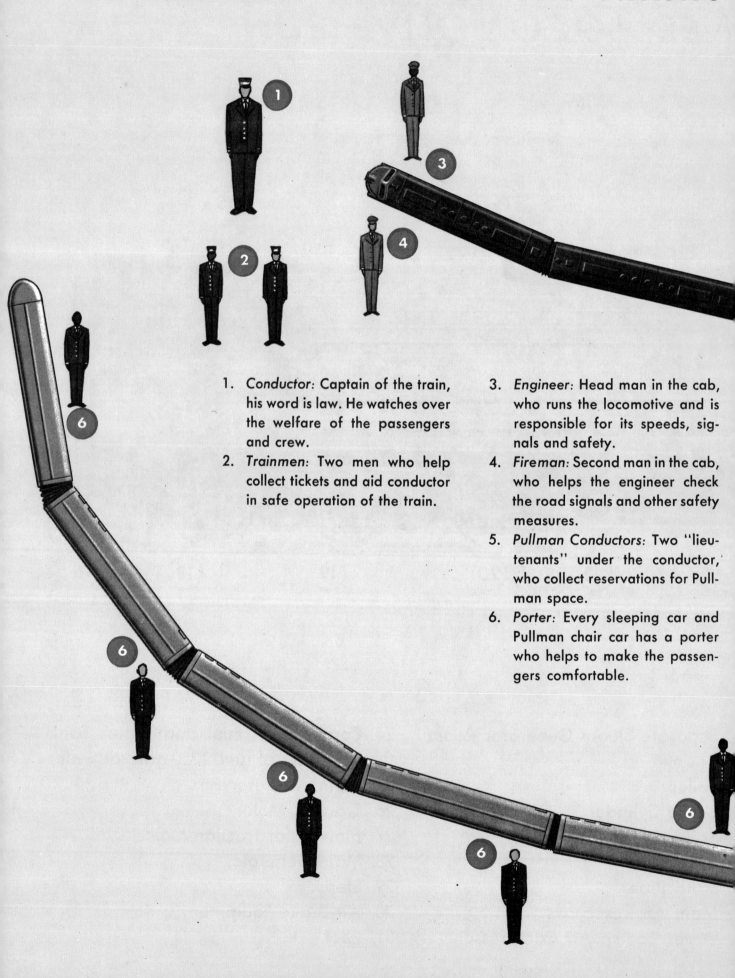

THE MEN WHO RUN THE TRAINS

1. *Conductor:* Captain of the train, his word is law. He watches over the welfare of the passengers and crew.
2. *Trainmen:* Two men who help collect tickets and aid conductor in safe operation of the train.
3. *Engineer:* Head man in the cab, who runs the locomotive and is responsible for its speeds, signals and safety.
4. *Fireman:* Second man in the cab, who helps the engineer check the road signals and other safety measures.
5. *Pullman Conductors:* Two "lieutenants" under the conductor, who collect reservations for Pullman space.
6. *Porter:* Every sleeping car and Pullman chair car has a porter who helps to make the passengers comfortable.

A crew of 38 men is required to perform the many services for safe, comfortable and convenient travel aboard a streamliner like the Pennsylvania Railroad's Congressional Limited. This drawing shows where each man is assigned.

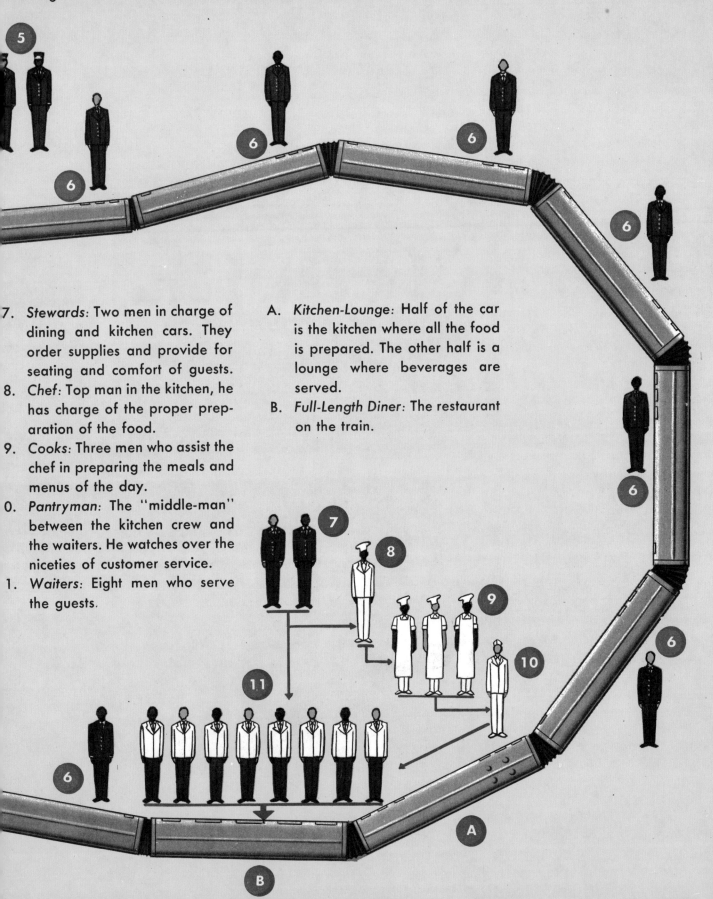

7. *Stewards:* Two men in charge of dining and kitchen cars. They order supplies and provide for seating and comfort of guests.
8. *Chef:* Top man in the kitchen, he has charge of the proper preparation of the food.
9. *Cooks:* Three men who assist the chef in preparing the meals and menus of the day.
0. *Pantryman:* The "middle-man" between the kitchen crew and the waiters. He watches over the niceties of customer service.
1. *Waiters:* Eight men who serve the guests.

A. *Kitchen-Lounge:* Half of the car is the kitchen where all the food is prepared. The other half is a lounge where beverages are served.
B. *Full-Length Diner:* The restaurant on the train.

FIRE ENGINES

E. ERNEST
PUBLISHER
G.J. ZAFFO
STUDIO
A. LEGGAT
INS.
JACOBS-
RUBIN
INC.
DR. BOOKER
X-RAY
P. & L. CIPES INC.
A. MULLEN FISH CO.
DRESSES

This big truck is a new kind of hook-and-ladder. It is easy to drive. It can turn in a narrow street. Look at the ladders. They are 65 to 100 feet long. They reach to high places.

Do you see the open cab in front of the truck? The driver sits in the open cab. He can see all around him. He can tell how much room he has to turn the truck.

The airport fire truck has a big water tank. It holds a lot of water.
The firemen on the truck can put out a fire in any part of the airport.
They use water from the big tank.

Some airport firemen use foam on the fire. The foam covers the fire. The airport truck carries many things to put out the fire. The truck is always ready to go to a fire.

The pumper pumps water. It pumps it from the hydrant. The pumper makes the water go faster through the hoses.

This fire engine can be used in any kind of weather. It is used mostly in .cold weather. Five men can sit in the closed cab. In cold weather the men are warm in the closed cab.

Do you see the large round outlet at the side of the truck? This is for the black hose. One end of the hose goes into the outlet. One end goes to the hydrant.

Do you see the two narrow water outlets above the large round one? These outlets are for white canvas hoses.

This pumper has an open cab. It is used mostly in warm weather. This pumper is very big. It pumps water much faster than the smaller pumper. A 14-foot ladder hangs on the side.

Do you see the outlets for the hoses? There are outlets on both sides of the truck. The firemen use the outlets on the side of the truck that is nearest to the hydrant.

A NIGHT WITH A

Night firemen have a large room in the firehouse. They sleep at home during the day. They stay in the firehouse at night. They are always ready to go to a fire.

1 At 6 o'clock in the evening the night fireman comes to the firehouse.

2 He lines up with other firemen to show that he is ready. He is told what to do.

5 The fireman runs to the pole as soon as he hears the bell. He slides down the pole. This is a quick way to get downstairs.

6 The fireman puts on his fire clothes in a hurry. He is ready to go to the fire.

9 Soon the fire is out. The fire chief calls out, "Shut down. Pick up. Go back to the firehouse." The firemen go back.

10 At the firehouse the firemen take off the used hose. They put on clean hose. They clean the fire engine.

13 The wet hose is hung in the drying room. The hose is long. Some hose is 50 feet long.

FIREMAN ON DUTY

3 The fireman goes upstairs. He changes into his working clothes.

4 A man turns in an alarm at a firebox. A bell rings in the fireman's room.

7 The fireman runs to the fire engine. Away he goes to the fire.

8 The firemen pull out the hose. They hook the pumper to the hydrant. They put water on the fire.

11 Soon the engine is clean. The fireman says, "The engine is ready to go to another fire."

12 Other firemen clean the used hose. They get it ready for the drying room.

14

At 8 o'clock the next morning the night fireman leaves the firehouse. He goes home to sleep. The day fireman takes his place at the firehouse.

Zaffo

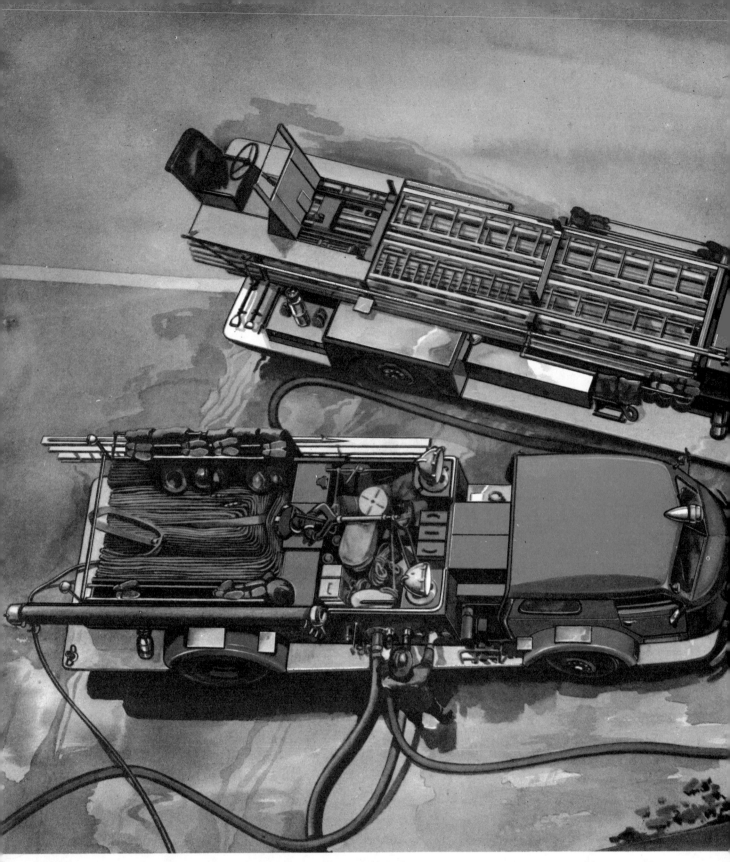

This hook-and-ladder is the biggest truck of all. This truck goes
out on big fires. A fireman sits in front and drives the truck. A fireman
sits in the back of the hook-and-ladder. He steers the rear wheels. The
two firemen work together to drive the hook-and-ladder.

Do you see the ladders? They can go up and down. They stop going up when the ladder touches the building.

The hook-and-ladder does not carry any hose. A pumper goes with the hook-and-ladder to carry the hose.

This fire engine is a hose truck. It goes out on all the fire alarms. Sometimes it goes with a hook-and-ladder. Sometimes it goes with a pumper. Sometimes it goes alone.

This fire engine carries hose on a reel. The hose goes to the 100-gallon tank of water. The hose truck also carries a first-aid box. This fire engine is a very useful one.

This truck is used in the country. The truck carries its own water in a big tank. It has two pumps on the front of the truck. It has many feet of canvas hose.

Look at the wheels on this fire engine. The back set of each group drives the truck. The truck can go over bumpy roads. It can go through fields where there are no roads.

THE FIRE ALARM

Follow the red arrows and see how it works.

1 FIREBOX (Closed)

This is the way a fire alarm box looks on a pole.
The number of this firebox is 3226.

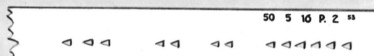

50 5 16 P. 2 53

3 RECORDER TAPE

This is the fire alarm recorder tape. The marks
tell the number of the firebox. The time and the
date are on the tape, too.

5 BELL

The bell will ring at a firehouse. It will ring at the
firehouse that is nearest to firebox 3226.

SYSTEM

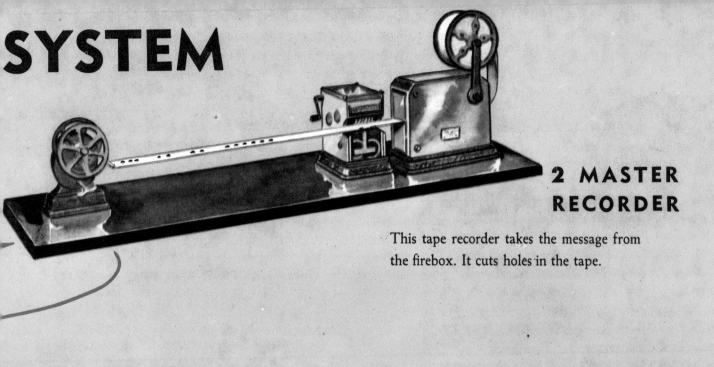

2 MASTER RECORDER

This tape recorder takes the message from the firebox. It cuts holes in the tape.

4 MANUAL TRANSMITTER

This transmitter sends the messages to the firehouses. It sends out the number of the box.

6 FIREBOX (Open)

The firemen go to the box. The person who sent the alarm should wait at the box. He should be there to tell the firemen where to go.

This truck is a kitchen on wheels. It goes to the fires with the fire engines. It carries food for the firemen. It goes out on large fires.

The field kitchen truck parks close to the fire. It does not get in the way of the firemen. This field kitchen truck is used in big cities.

The Fire Chief has a red car. He uses the car to hurry to all the fires. The siren makes a loud noise. Then all the other cars stop.

Sometimes the Fire Chief does not drive fast. He does not use the siren. His red car goes along with the other cars on the street.

BOATS
and
SHIPS

TUGBOAT • Big ships are too clumsy to go alone into or out of their places alongside piers. They need small boats to help them. Tugboats do this work. They can nose their padded bows against a ship and push very hard. They can pull very hard, too. They often pull whole strings of flat-bottomed boats, called barges, carrying heavy loads of coal, sand, or even railroad cars.

Seagoing tugs are big and strong enough to travel over the ocean. Other tugs

are built very low so that they can pull canal barges under bridges. The tug shown here is a harbor tug. It has a crew of seven men. The captain is in charge. The mate helps him. A deckhand takes care of the tug's big ropes. The chief engineer has charge of the engines. The oiler oils them and keeps the engine room clean. The fireman feeds the engines fuel. And, of course, there is a cook who makes chow for the whole crew.

SUBMARINE • The nuclear-powered attack submarine shown here is the U.S.S. "Skipjack." A true submarine, the "Skipjack" can go all around the world under water. It can travel over 100,000 miles before it needs refueling. Some nuclear subs can dive to a depth of over 400 feet and some can fire missiles while under the surface. Officers and sailors have stayed aboard under water for as long as 83 days before returning to the surface.

This is how a sub dives: She has tanks which can be filled with air or water. When there is air in the tanks, she floats on the surface. When there is water in the tanks, she becomes too heavy to float, so she goes down under the surface. The hydro-wings on the fin (the fin was once called the conning tower) and the stern (rear) control planes are used like the controls on an airplane. To see on the surface while under water, a sub uses a periscope.

THE FIRST BOAT. Nobody knows what the first boat in the world looked like. But we can guess that people began to travel across water by holding onto a log and paddling with one arm.

OUTRIGGER. We do know that long, long ago, men discovered they could get around better if they hollowed out a log and sat inside. To keep the "boat" from tipping over, they sometimes fastened smaller logs on each side. Boats with these balancers are still used. They are called outriggers.

VIKING SHIP. Still later, men discovered how useful oars can be. And then they found out about sails. Here is a Viking long ship that has both oars and a sail. The Vikings were fearless seamen, and they sailed across the Atlantic Ocean even before Columbus did.

"SANTA MARIA." By the time Columbus came, men knew that ships could travel without oars if they had enough sails, and could carry cargo, too. Here is the "Santa Maria," one of the three boats in which Columbus and his men sailed.

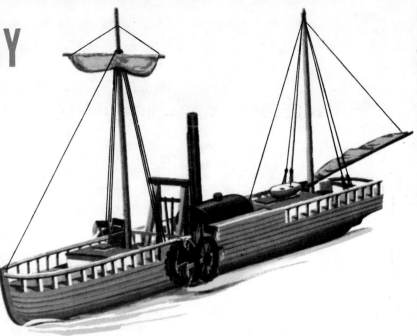

"CLERMONT." This is the first steamboat, which Robert Fulton built and ran up the Hudson River from New York to Albany. People along the banks ran away in fright when they saw the noisy, smoky vessel coming along without sails.

"MAYFLOWER." Sailing ships became bigger and bigger as men learned more about building them. This is the famous ship which brought the Pilgrims to America.

AMERICAN CLIPPER. Even after steamboats were invented, men kept on making faster and better sailing ships. American clipper ships like the "Rainbow," shown here, were the fastest of all, and they won many races, sailing halfway around the world, carrying valuable cargoes.

IRONCLAD WARSHIPS. These two warships were made of wood covered with iron. They fought one of the famous sea battles of the Civil War. The "Monitor," flying the American flag, was nicknamed a "cheese box on a raft." She defeated the "Merrimac," which belonged to the South.

CARGO VESSEL • Ships that carry heavy loads of freight are called cargo vessels or freighters. If you know a lot about them, you can tell the different models, just as you can tell one automobile from another. The "Sea Serpent," shown here, is a C2-S-B1. The cargo is stored deep down inside the ship in big rooms called holds. Derricks on the ship, which are called booms, pick up the cargo from the pier and lower it into the holds through hatches, which are openings in the deck.

The booms are the long, slender poles sticking up and out, with ropes and pulleys dangling from them. When a freighter is at sea, these booms are tied down close to the deck so they won't swing around. Sailors call this "cradling" the booms. The big posts which hold the booms up are called king posts or Samson posts. Sometimes sailors call them goal posts, because they look like goal posts on a football field. On some freighters, masts instead of king posts hold up the booms.

WHISTLE SIGNALS

 If a vessel is turning to starboard (right), it gives one short blast on its whistle.

 If it is turning to port (left), a vessel gives two short blasts on its whistle.

Three short blasts mean a vessel is backing up.

Four short blasts mean "Danger!"

 A vessel gives one long blast to warn other vessels that it is about to leave a pier.

When a vessel gives three long blasts, it is just saying "Hello!" to some other vessel.

 A vessel blows its whistle only when it wants to give a signal to other vessels. And other vessels always show that they have heard the signal by answering with the same signal on their own whistles.

As you know, there are right-of-way rules for automobiles at crossings. The rules tell which cars have to stop and let the others go ahead first. Vessels have right-of-way rules, too. Look at the shaded part of the round picture. The vessel in the shaded part has the right of way over the vessels in the white part. Only the shaded part is a danger zone for the vessel in the center. It has the right of way over other vessels in the white part. All the other vessels have danger zones on their starboard (right) sides, too.

HOW, WHEN AND WHY THE SHIP'S BELL IS STRUCK

1 BELL

2 BELLS

3 BELLS

4 BELLS

5 BELLS

6 BELLS

7 BELLS

8 BELLS

Starting with three bells, the bell is struck in pairs, with a short pause before additional bells (strokes) are struck.

There are six tours of watch duty on board a vessel, each one four hours long. The first watch starts at 8:00 P.M. and ends at midnight. At 8:30, one stroke on the ship's bell indicates that the first half hour of the watch has been completed. An additional bell is struck for each succeeding half hour, so that when midnight comes, eight bells are struck. Then the next four-hour watch starts, and the bells begin all over again. One bell means 12:30 A.M., and so on, up to eight bells, which now mean it is 4 A.M.

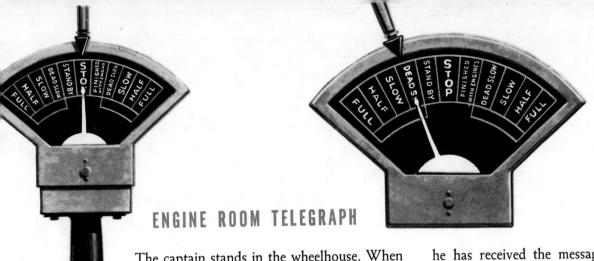

ENGINE ROOM TELEGRAPH

The captain stands in the wheelhouse. When he wants the ship to go faster or slower, or stop, or back up, he gives the order to the chief engineer, who is way down inside the ship, in the engine room. The captain signals the engineer on the engine room telegraph.

If the captain wishes the ship to stop, he pushes the handle on his telegraph until it points to STOP. The engineer has his telegraph down in the engine room. To show he has received the message, he pushes *his* handle to STOP. This moves the white arrow on the captain's telegraph to STOP. When the handle and the arrow are lined up, the captain knows the engineer has received his order. If the captain wants the ship to go ahead slowly, he pushes the handle to DEAD SLOW, on the left side of the telegraph. If he wants it to back up slowly, he pushes the handle to DEAD SLOW on the right.

INTERNATIONAL CODE FLAG SIGNALS

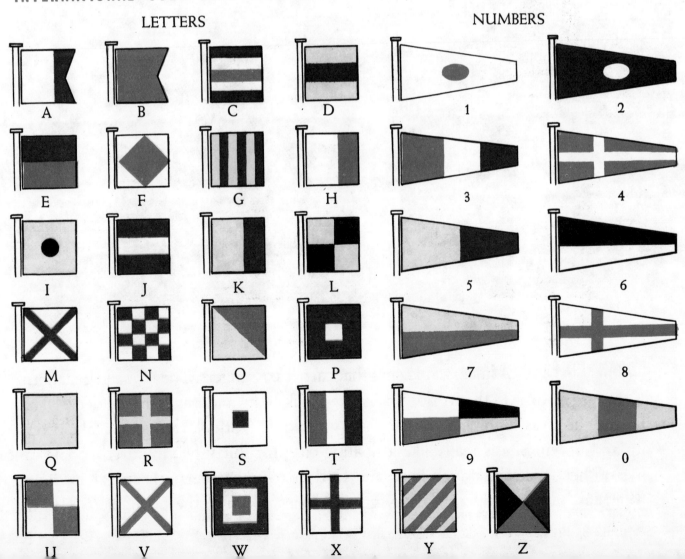

LETTERS   NUMBERS

A B C D 1 2
E F G H 3 4
I J K L 5 6
M N O P 7 8
Q R S T 9 0
U V W X Y Z

OCEAN LINER • A liner is a big ship that carries passengers. The "Queen Elizabeth" is the largest liner in the world. She is five blocks long and has fourteen decks. That means she is as high as a fourteen-story building, with elevators that take people up and down. She is really like a floating city, for thirty-five hundred people can live on her while she travels back and forth across the ocean. They eat in dining rooms as big as restaurants. They go to movies, swim in the pool, exercise in the

gym, and play games on the decks. Children have a special room to play in. There is a barbershop for the men and a beauty parlor for the women. Even the dogs have an exercise deck, all their own!

There is so much work to do on the "Queen Elizabeth" that it takes twelve hundred people to do it. There is even work for radio-telephone operators, who can connect you with any number you want to call almost anywhere in the world.

SMALL CRAFT

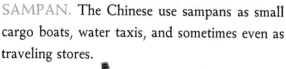

LIFEBOAT. If a ship is sinking, people get into lifeboats, lower them to the water, and escape. The lifeboat shown here is a motorboat. The man is holding the rudder used to steer the boat.

SAMPAN. The Chinese use sampans as small cargo boats, water taxis, and sometimes even as traveling stores.

SCULL. This is a very light boat, built to go very fast and used mostly for racing.

ROWBOAT. A rowboat is a sturdy boat rowed with oars. The small rowboat you often see being towed behind a sailing vessel or motorboat is called a dinghy.

KAYAK. An Eskimo makes his kayak of animal skin. He laces the opening tightly around his waist to keep water out.

LIFE RAFT. Many ships carry air-filled rubber rafts to which shipwrecked people can cling till help comes.

SAILING DINGHY. This is the name for a dinghy that carries a sail as well as oars.

CANOE. Indians invented the canoe, which they made of bark. Today, many canoes are made of waterproofed canvas.

OUTBOARD RACER. A noisy motor with a propeller, which is attached at the stern of this small boat, pushes the boat through the water very fast.

ODD CRAFT

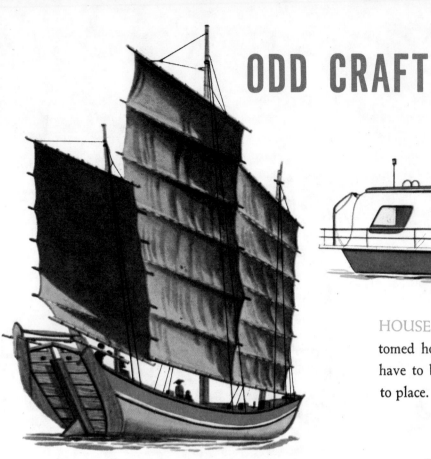

HOUSEBOAT. Many people live on flat-bottomed houseboats like this one. But the boats have to be towed in order to move from place to place.

JUNK. The captain of this Chinese cargo vessel lives on board with not only his whole family, but even with his chickens and ducks.

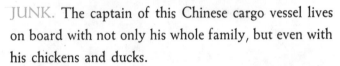

HYDROPLANE A propeller in the air instead of in the water makes a hydroplane go.

CATAMARAN. Gar Wood, a famous motorboat builder and racer, designed this craft, which is modeled after fast South Sea sailboats called catamarans.

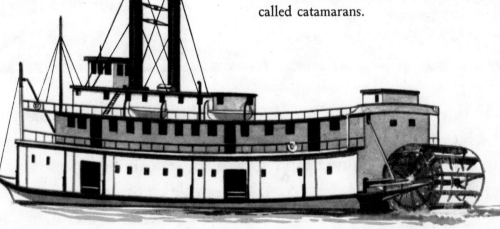

RIVER BOAT. Boats like this travel up and down the Mississippi River. Called stern-wheelers, they

have a big wheel that pushes them from behind, instead of paddle wheels at the sides.

FIREBOAT • Here is the "Firefighter," the biggest fireboat in the world, trying to save a burning freighter. All her nozzles together can shoot out as much water as twenty fire engines could on land. One big nozzle in the bow squirts enough water in a minute to fill a swimming pool. The nozzle on the tower shoots farther than the others. It can aim water at the deck of the freighter or even down into the hold.

Most big seaports have at least one fireboat. New York City has ten. They

fight fires along the waterfront, when piers are burning or when vessels catch fire. They sometimes help firemen on land by pumping water to them. And they even go out to sea, where they help ships that have radioed that they are burning. Because of the dangerous machinery used, seagoing firemen cannot have mascots.

Tugboats like the one shown here near the "Firefighter" can fight fires, too. Many of them have a nozzle high up in the bow, which can be used in emergencies.

PARTS OF A DUAL-ENGINE CRUISER. This is a small dual-engine cruiser which people use mostly for fun. But the names of the parts you see here are used on all kinds of boats and ships.

1. ENSIGN
2. MOORING BITTS
3. STERN DECK
4. STERN HATCH
5. COMPANIONWAY DOOR TO AFT CABIN
6. FLYING BRIDGE DECK
7. PORT SIDE (left side)
8. STEERING WHEEL
9. CONTROL PANEL
10. 32-POINT WHITE RANGE LIGHT
11. HAND THROTTLE
12. WINDSHIELD
13. HORN
14. RED PORT SIDE LIGHT (10 points)
15. HANDRAILS
16. GREEN STARBOARD SIDE LIGHT (10 points)
17. FORWARD HATCH
18. ANCHOR
19. PENNANT
20. 20-POINT WHITE BOW RANGE LIGHT

21. BOW (front of boat)
22. PORTHOLES
23. DECKHOUSE
24. DRAFT
25. STARBOARD SIDE (right side)
26. VENTILATORS
27. CORK RING BUOYS (lifesavers)
28. AFT CABIN
29. LINE CLEATS
30. VENTILATOR
31. EXHAUST PIPES
32. PROPELLERS
33. RUDDERS
34. STERN (back of boat)

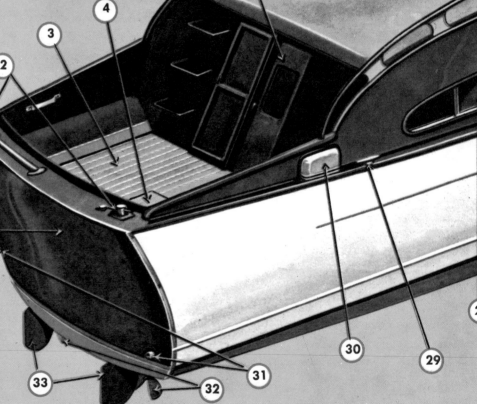

RANGE LIGHTS

At night a vessel turns on white lights which are called range lights. The front (bow) light is always lower than the rear (stern) light. Each vessel also has a red light on its left (port) side and a green light on its right (starboard) side. These are called running lights. Anyone seeing them can tell in which direction the vessel is moving.

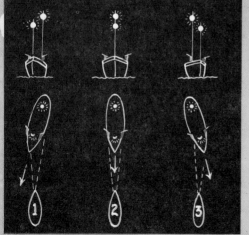

The diagram at the left shows how lights keep vessels from ramming each other at night. Imagine you are in vessel No. 1. You see both red and green lights ahead. This means a vessel is coming toward you. (Colored lights and the bow range lights are fixed so that you can't see them from behind.) Now look at the range lights. The lower or bow light is at your left. So you know the vessel is headed toward your left (port) side. Now imagine you're in vessel No. 2. You see red and green lights. The range lights are in a straight line up and down. You know the other vessel is coming straight toward you. If you are in vessel No. 3, the lower range light is to the right of the higher one. The other vessel is headed to your right (starboard) side.

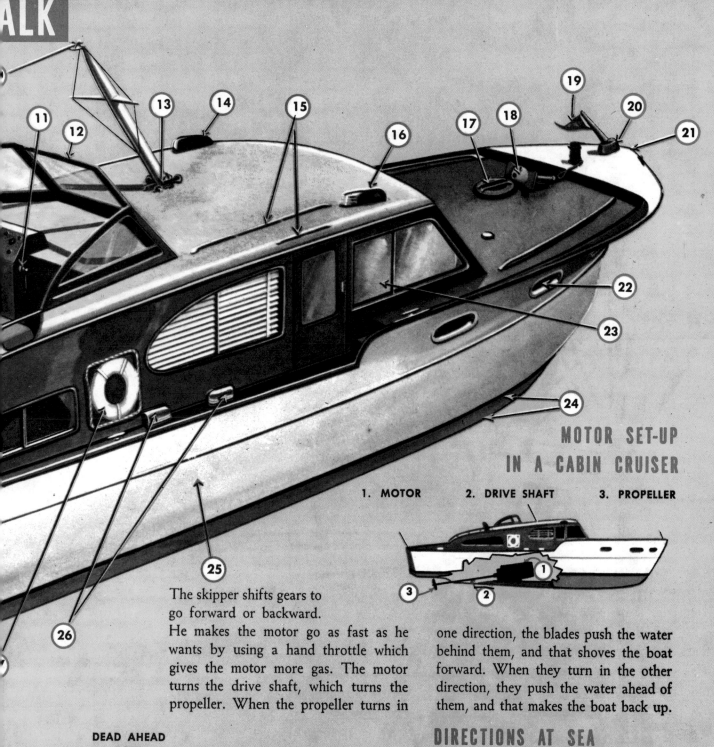

The skipper shifts gears to go forward or backward. He makes the motor go as fast as he wants by using a hand throttle which gives the motor more gas. The motor turns the drive shaft, which turns the propeller. When the propeller turns in one direction, the blades push the water behind them, and that shoves the boat forward. When they turn in the other direction, they push the water ahead of them, and that makes the boat back up.

MOTOR SET-UP IN A CABIN CRUISER

1. MOTOR   2. DRIVE SHAFT   3. PROPELLER

DIRECTIONS AT SEA

If a sailor standing in the center of a vessel sees another vessel straight ahead of him, he says it is *dead ahead*. If he sees a vessel way behind him on the left, he says it is on *the port quarter*. The chart at the left shows other words used to describe direction. These points also divide the lights.

White stern range light (in back) shines in all directions. It is called a 32-point light, because the compass sailors use has 32 points, or directions, marked on it.

White bow range light (in front) shines a little more than halfway around. A 20-point light, it is visible from dead ahead to two points abaft the beam on either side.

Red port side light (left) is a 10-point light. It is visible from dead ahead to two points abaft the port beam.

Green starboard side light (right) is a 10-point light, visible from dead ahead to two points abaft the starboard beam.

DEAD AHEAD
BOW

RT BOW   STARBOARD BOW

ARD OF THE   FORWARD OF THE
BEAM   STARBOARD BEAM
E   ON THE
BEAM   STARBOARD BEAM

T THE   ABAFT THE
BEAM   STARBOARD BEAM

N THE   ON THE
RT QUARTER   STARBOARD QUARTER

DEAD ASTERN

STERN

(THE CENTER IS MIDSHIPS.)

SAILBOATS • People have sailboats mainly for fun. They take cruises in them along the seacoasts or on big lakes. Sometimes they race each other, and the boats skim over the water at high speed, with nothing but the wind filling the sails to push them.

The boats in this picture are yawls. The sail over the bow of the yawl is a jib. The sail by the big mast is the mainsail, and the little one in the stern is the mizzen sail. Yawls come in different sizes, but usually they are big enough to have bunks

for people to sleep in and a galley where they can cook. There are many other kinds of sailboats, too. You can tell them apart by the types of sails they have.

The buoy at the left guides vessels near shore. It has a light at the top and four bells down below. The buoy floats on the water, though actually it is anchored in one place. Night or day, and in fog, too, vessels can tell where they are by the sight or sound of the buoys.

AIRCRAFT CARRIER • An aircraft carrier is really an airfield that can move all around the world on the ocean. Airplanes are stored inside the carrier with their wings folded up. Elevators take the folded planes up to the top deck, called the flight deck. There, men straighten the wings out, and the planes are ready to fly.

Every airplane on the carrier has a hook near its tail. When the plane lands, this hook catches onto what is called the arresting gear, on the flight deck This stops

the plane, the way you would stop a flying bird if you caught its feet and held them tight. If a plane does fall into the water, the carrier sends out a special little boat, called a crash boat, to rescue the flier and bring him back.

The officers run the carrier from a tower, called the Island, located on the starboard side of the flight deck. Inside the carrier, the sailors have dining rooms, places to sleep, a laundry where they wash clothes, and even soda fountains.

BUILDING and WRECKING MACHINES

BULLDOZER • A bulldozer is a large tractor on crawlers, with a steel blade attached to the front. It has tremendous pushing and pulling power. For this reason, the bulldozer is especially valuable in making roadbeds. After the dump trucks or scrapers have unloaded gravel or earth, the bulldozer pushes it to where it is needed. The driver can raise the blade a little to help spread out the gravel or earth after it has been moved. The bulldozer is also used to open roads for traffic after a heavy snowstorm, or to level off

land for lawns or tennis courts. Sometimes it is used to clear large areas of small trees.

A boom can be attached to the front, and the bulldozer can then be used as a small crane. An attachment for lifting can also be hooked up to the front, and then the bulldozer is used to help load trucks. This bulldozer has a hood over the driver's seat to protect him from bad weather. Farmers, loggers, contractors and the Armed Services all use bulldozers to help them in their work.

TAMPING-LEVELING FINISHER • The tamping-leveling finisher is used to pave new streets with asphalt, or to repave old streets. A dump truck loads the hopper with as much as five tons of asphalt. As the finisher crawls along, it spreads the asphalt. It automatically measures the correct amount of asphalt over the road so as to leave a level surface. If there are low spots, the finisher pours more asphalt there than on the rest of the surface. On the extreme opposite ends of the finisher are

the leveling arms, used to control the matching of the asphalt strips. After one strip has been laid, the leveling arm is set so that the next strip will match it exactly. The man at the left is making this adjustment. In this picture, the driver is sitting on the other side. Normally, however, the driver sits on the same side that is to be matched, so that he can control the machine better along the matching line. Two complete sets of controls on the finisher allow the driver to operate the machine from either side.

BUCKET LOADER • The bucket loader is used for loading different kinds
of building materials onto a dump truck. It can load earth, gravel, sand and other bulky
materials, such as snow. The bucket loader can also be used to clean up large areas of
ground, or to level off surfaces. It has special wheels so that it can be moved easily, and
it can be towed behind any dump truck. The bucket loader has small buckets spaced one
foot apart that run along a roller chain. At the very bottom is a spiral bucket feeder that

looks like two huge corkscrews. As the spiral bucket feeder spins, it churns up the material. When the bottom bucket passes through the material, it loads itself and then moves up the roller chain. In this way, each bucket loads itself and moves up the chain. When the buckets reach the top of the elevator, they roll over and are emptied into a chute called the boom. The boom is directed so that the material falls squarely into the dump truck, and can then be carted off to where it is needed.

THREE-AXLE TANDEM ROLLER • In road building, the roller
goes to work after the asphalt has been laid down. The roller is driven back and forth
over the asphalt to smooth it out. It is the driver's responsibility to see that there are no
bumps left on the road for automobile drivers to complain about.

The driver of the three-axle tandem roller rides backward. He has to make certain
that the area he has just rolled is smooth and matches the rest of the surface. Of course,

the driver sometimes turns around to see what is going on in front of him, too.

The three-axle tandem roller does an excellent job of smoothing out rough spots in the road. When the first roller goes over the bump, it lifts that roller off the surface of the road. The weight of the first roller is then transferred to the two remaining rollers, giving them additional weight and strength. If the second roller doesn't smooth out the high spot, the third roller surely will.

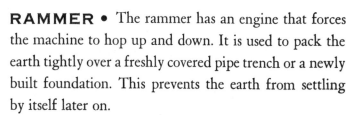

WATER PUMP • A water pump is used to lift water from foundations. Sometimes builders strike water when they dig very deep; or a hard rain may flood the foundation. Then the water pump goes into action. It can pump out seven thousand gallons of water in one hour.

RAMMER • The rammer has an engine that forces the machine to hop up and down. It is used to pack the earth tightly over a freshly covered pipe trench or a newly built foundation. This prevents the earth from settling by itself later on.

POWER WHEELBARROW • This is a wheelbarrow with an engine. The man operating this wheelbarrow does not have to lift it up at all, enabling him to do much more work in a day. After the wheelbarrow has been fully loaded and taken to the place where it is needed, the man touches the foot pedal and the tub tilts forward and unloads itself.

OWER TOOLS

JACK HAMMER • The jack hammer is used to break concrete walls, concrete roads or any other tough surface. It is also used to drill holes in rock. It is powered by compressed air forced from the compressor at the left, through the air-hose line and into the machine. The jack hammer makes a lot of noise when it is hard at work.

POWER SAW • The power saw can cut through several boards very quickly. For example, if a carpenter is building a floor and there are many boards of different lengths sticking over the edge, he uses a power saw to cut them all off to the same length. The power saw can also cut through boards at an angle.

VIBRATOR • The vibrator is used to force the freshly poured concrete into all corners of a mold. Its action is something like that of an egg beater. When the vibrator is thrust into the liquid concrete, it shakes the mixture until all the little empty air pockets in the concrete are filled. The concrete then settles into a good solid, strong mass.

ROCK CRUSHER • The rock crusher can crush large pieces of rock to almost any size. The one shown here is the type usually used in quarries, where it is necessary to crush large quantities of hard rock. The rock is fed from the hopper into the jaw crusher, where it is broken into pieces. This particular rock crusher is able to crush and screen the rock into three different sizes at the same time. In this picture all the rock is being crushed to approximately one size, but it is also being screened. Small

pieces which chip off drop through the screen, and are not discharged. The rest pours out of the conveyor at the right, into a truck. If the rock were being crushed to three sizes, there would be three conveyors discharging crushed rock.

The rock crusher is mounted on twelve wheels, and can be hooked up to a tractor truck or a bulldozer and moved over highways, or over rough ground. There are also small portable rock crushers which are used on highways to crush rock for roadbeds.

MOTO-CRANE • Like any crane, the moto-crane is used for loading, lifting and wrecking. However, it runs on wheels instead of crawlers, so that it can be driven along the highways to the area where it is needed. It is used on jobs that cover large areas, or on widely separated small jobs. Oversized "doughnut" tires permit the moto-crane to travel on soft ground and even on desert sand. Different attachments such as buckets, grapples, tongs, clamps, slings, hooks and magnets are put on the end of the

long boom, depending upon the job the moto-crane must do. In this picture the moto-crane is loading pipes onto a freight car with an attachment called a sling. One of the most interesting attachments is the magnet, often used to load scrap metal. The boom with the magnet slides over the scrap. Electricity driven into the magnet then pulls the scrap toward it. The scrap will cling to the magnet while the driver swings the boom to where he wants to unload. Then he turns off the electricity and the scrap drops off.

MOTOR GRADER

The motor grader is used on farms to make ditches, and in road building to level off uneven surfaces, slope banks and widen streets. In the winter the motor grader can be used as a snowplow. This picture shows the motor grader leveling off a roadbed which eventually will become a smooth concrete highway.

The wheels are made so that the motor grader can move on tilted surfaces. When it moves, it looks like a caterpillar bumping along rough ground. The long gooseneck

between the driver's cabin and the front wheels is necessary in order to leave enough room for the steel grading blade. The blade is located behind the front wheels. The driver can swing the blade in any direction, and he can also raise or lower it. An attachment called a scarifier can be hooked up directly in front of the blade. This has sharp teeth, which dig into tough, uneven surfaces and loosen the earth so that the blade can level it down easily.

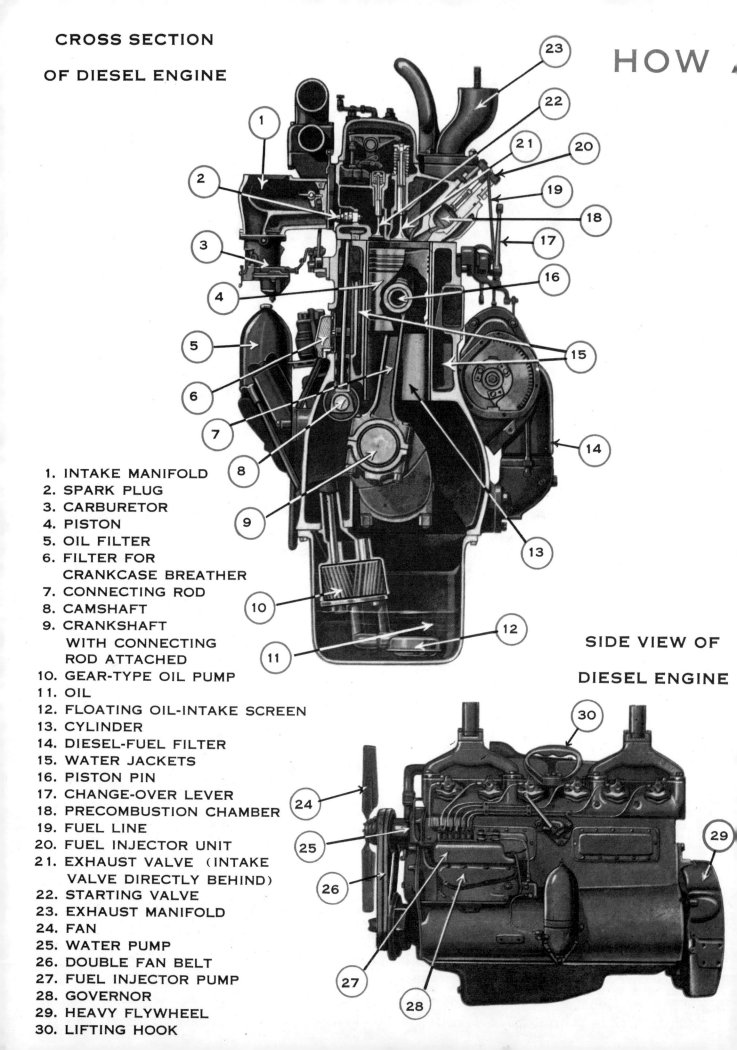

SIDE VIEW OF

DIESEL ENGINE

1. INTAKE MANIFOLD
2. SPARK PLUG
3. CARBURETOR
4. PISTON
5. OIL FILTER
6. FILTER FOR
   CRANKCASE BREATHER
7. CONNECTING ROD
8. CAMSHAFT
9. CRANKSHAFT
   WITH CONNECTING
   ROD ATTACHED
10. GEAR-TYPE OIL PUMP
11. OIL
12. FLOATING OIL-INTAKE SCREEN
13. CYLINDER
14. DIESEL-FUEL FILTER
15. WATER JACKETS
16. PISTON PIN
17. CHANGE-OVER LEVER
18. PRECOMBUSTION CHAMBER
19. FUEL LINE
20. FUEL INJECTOR UNIT
21. EXHAUST VALVE (INTAKE
    VALVE DIRECTLY BEHIND)
22. STARTING VALVE
23. EXHAUST MANIFOLD
24. FAN
25. WATER PUMP
26. DOUBLE FAN BELT
27. FUEL INJECTOR PUMP
28. GOVERNOR
29. HEAVY FLYWHEEL
30. LIFTING HOOK

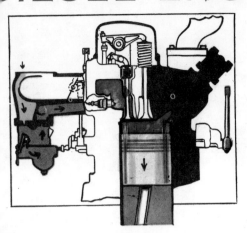

A Diesel operates on oil fired not by a spark, but by compression heat. Therefore, a cold Diesel must be started by some other power source in order to warm up the engine for Diesel fuel. Here, it is started with gasoline in the auxiliary combustion chamber (shown in black in pictures 1, 2, 3, and 4). With the change-over lever in "start" position, the Diesel part (shown in black in picture at left) is not working. After a minute, the change-over switches the engine to Diesel operation and the gasoline part stops working.

A DIESEL POWER CYCLE

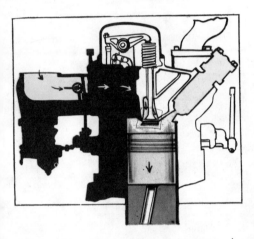

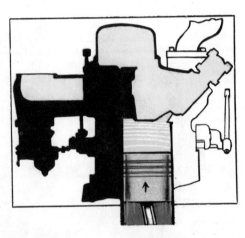

1. INTAKE STROKE • The intake valve opens and the piston goes down. In this view the intake valve (with head shown in red) is located directly behind the exhaust valve. On the intake stroke a Diesel sucks in air alone (shown in blue, above), unlike a gasoline engine, which draws in a fuel-air mixture.

2. COMPRESSION STROKE • Now all valves are closed and the piston rises, greatly compressing the air inside. The temperature of the air charge is suddenly boosted.

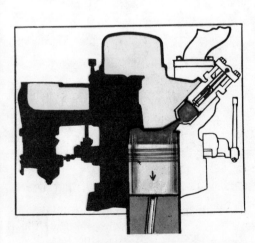

3. POWER STROKE • As the piston nears top dead center, oil is injected in a spray and is ignited by compression heat. This forces the piston down, giving power to the crankshaft.

4. EXHAUST STROKE • The exhaust valve (here shown in red) opens and the piston starts its last upstroke of the cycle, forcing the burned gases into the exhaust manifold. At the top of its stroke, the piston begins the cycle again.

MOTOR SCRAPER

MOTOR SCRAPER • Before the motor scraper was invented, a contractor had to hire many men to load a dump truck with hand shovels in order to move earth from one spot to another. Now, a motor scraper, with one operator, loads the earth, moves it to where it is needed and dumps it. Actually, the motor scraper consists of a two-wheeled tractor joined to a two-wheeled scraper. The extra-large tires are made so that the scraper can be used on all kinds of ground. The powerful motor scraper is used only

when the material it is carrying is to be unloaded near the spot where it is picked up.

The motor scraper works like a carpet sweeper. It rides over the earth that it is going to remove, and the driver drops the powerful jaws into cutting position. The machine is loaded with earth, and when it is full the driver closes the jaws and the scraper moves on to where it will unload. This is all done in one continual motion. The scraper does not have to stop during any stage of its loading or unloading.

CONCRETE MIXER WITH CRANE • This is a special kind

of cement and concrete mixer with a crane attachment. It is used to pour cement or
concrete into places where the flow must be controlled so that it does not spill over. The
mixer lays the concrete for roads, and it pours concrete into foundation forms for drains,
tunnels and other building projects. Trucks dump the dry mixture into the skip, shown
at the bottom left in this picture. The skip is then lifted up so that the mixture drops

into the big drum on the top of the mixer. The drum revolves, and as it turns, water is fed into the drum. When the concrete is properly mixed with the water, it is released from the drum into the clamshell bucket, which then rides along the boom rail. The clamshell-bucket door opens and unloads the concrete slowly. The boom can be raised as high as twenty-one feet, so the concrete can be poured into trucks, or into forms high above the ground. One man operates the mixer from a platform over the rear wheels.

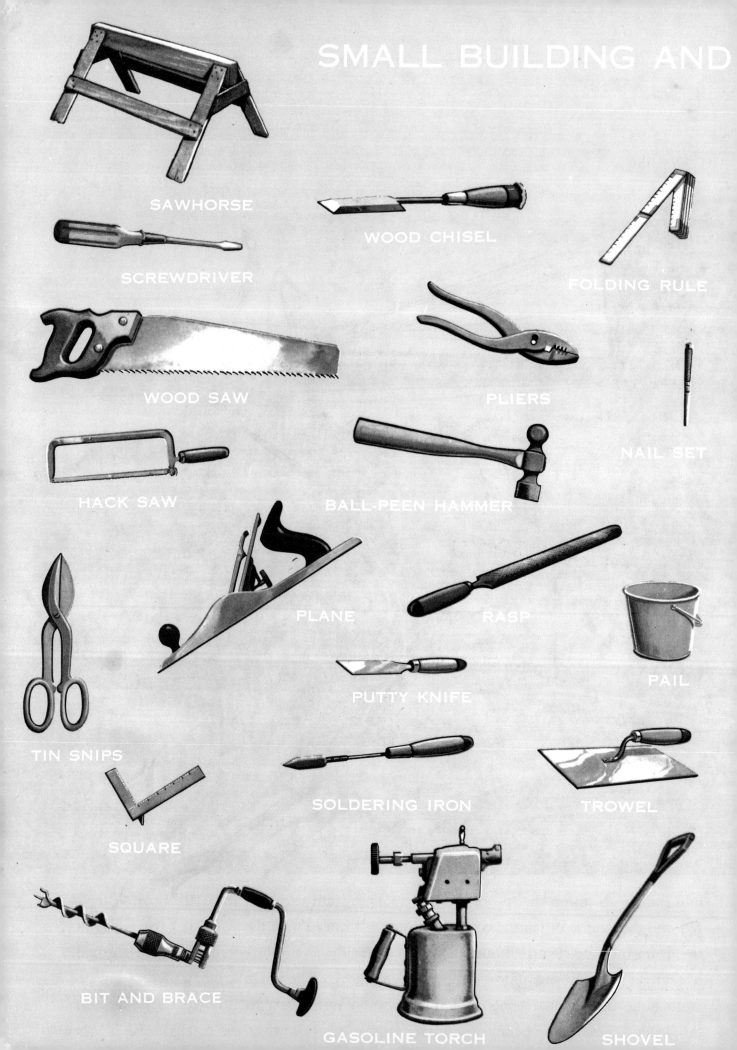

SMALL BUILDING AND

SAWHORSE

WOOD CHISEL

FOLDING RULE

SCREWDRIVER

PLIERS

WOOD SAW

NAIL SET

HACK SAW

BALL-PEEN HAMMER

PLANE

RASP

PAIL

PUTTY KNIFE

TIN SNIPS

SOLDERING IRON

TROWEL

SQUARE

BIT AND BRACE

GASOLINE TORCH

SHOVEL